Excel 4

by Seta Krikorian Frantz

A Division of Prentice Hall Computer Publishing
11711 North College Avenue, Carmel, Indiana 46032 USA

To my parents. Thank you for all of your love and support. I love you.

© 1993 by Alpha Books

All rights reserved. No part of this book shall be reproduced, stored in a retrieval system, or transmitted by any means, electronic, mechanical, photocopying, recording, or otherwise, without written permission from the publisher. No patent liability is assumed with respect to the use of the information contained herein. Although every precaution has been taken in the preparation of this book, the publisher and author assume no responsibility for errors or omissions. Neither is any liability assumed for damages resulting from the use of the information contained herein. For information, address Alpha Books, 11711 North College Avenue, Carmel, IN 46032

International Standard Book Number: 1-56761-186-9
Library of Congress Catalog Card Number: 93-70366

95 94 93   8 7 6 5 4 3 2 1

Interpretation of the printing code: the rightmost number of the first series of numbers is the year of the book's printing; the rightmost number of the second series of numbers is the number of the book's printing. For example, a printing code of 93-1 shows that the first printing of the book occurred in 1993.

Screen reproductions in this book were created by means of the program Collage Plus from Inner Media, Inc., Hollis, NH.

Printed in the United States of America

Publisher: *Marie Butler-Knight*
Associate Publisher: *Lisa A. Bucki*
Managing Editor: *Elizabeth Keaffaber*
Acquisitions Manager: *Stephen R. Poland*
Manuscript Editor: *Barry Childs-Helton*
Cover Designer: *Jay Corpus*
Designer: *Amy Peppler-Adams*
Indexer: *Jeanne Clark*
Production Team: *Diana Bigham, Tim Cox, Mark Enochs, Tom Loveman, Joe Ramon, Carrie Roth, Barbara Webster*

Special thanks to Kelly Oliver for ensuring the technical accuracy of this book.

The text in this book is printed on recycled paper.

One Minute Reference Excel 4

Contents

Introduction vii
Conventions Used in This Book vii
Trademarks ix

Microsoft Excel Basics x

Cell—Adding Borders 1
Cell—Deleting 3
Cell—Goto 5
Cell—Inserting 6
Cell—Selecting 8
Cell—Showing Active Cell 8
Cell Notes—Adding 9
Cell Notes—Viewing, Editing or Deleting 11
Chart—Activating 12
Chart—Arrow—Adding 13
Chart—Arrow—Deleting 14
Chart—Attaching Text 15
Chart—Axes 16
Chart—Calculate Now 17
Chart—Color Palette—Changing 18
Chart—Creating with ChartWizard 20
Chart—Creating with Toolbar 21
Chart—Creating in Separate Document 22
Chart—Editing Series 24
Chart—Formatting 3-D View 26
Chart—Formatting Main Chart 27
Chart—Gallery 30
Chart—Gridlines 32
Chart—Legend—Adding 33
Chart—Legend—Deleting 35
Chart—Moving and Sizing Embedded 36
Chart—Moving Object 36
Chart—Overlay—Adding 37
Chart—Overlay—Deleting 38
Chart—Protecting Documents 39
Chart—Scaling 40
Chart—Selecting Entire 42
Chart—Sizing Objects 43

Chart—Unprotecting 44
Column—Changing Width 45
Column—Deleting 47
Column—Inserting 47

Data—Aligning Data 47
Data—Changing Font, Style, Size, Color
and Effects 49
Data—Clearing 51
Data—Copying 53
Data—Cutting and Moving 56
Data—Finding and Replacing 58
Data—Insert Paste 61
Data—Pasting 62
Data—Protecting 64
Data—Styles 66
Data Form 68
Database—Defining 69
Database—Defining an Extract Range 71
Database—Deleting Records 72
Database—Extracting Data 74
Database—Finding Data 75
Database—Setting Criteria 76
Database—Sorting Records 79
Display Options—Setting 82

Exiting 84

File—Closing 85
File—Closing All 86
File—Deleting 86
File—New 88
File—Opening 89
File—Save 91
File—Saving with a New Name 92
Formula—Creating 94
Formula—Using Absolute References 97
Formula—Using Relative References 99
Formula—Goal Seeking 100
Formula—Pasting Functions 102
Formula—Pasting Names 104
Formula—Protecting 105
Formula—Setting Calculation Options 105
Formula—Solver 108

Graphic Object—Bringing to Front 111
Graphic Object—Copying 111
Graphic Object—Creating 112
Graphic Object—Deleting 112
Graphic Object—Formatting 112
Graphic Object—Grouping 114
Graphic Object—Moving 114
Graphic Object—Selecting 115
Graphic Object—Sending to Back 115

Links—Creating 116
Links—Updating 118

Macro—Pausing Recording 119
Macro—Recording 120
Macro—Resuming Recording 122
Macro—Running 123
Menu Commands—Selecting 124

Number—Formatting 125

OLE Object—Creating 128
OLE Object—Editing 130
OLE Object—Selecting 130
Outline—Creating 131

Page Breaks—Automatic 132
Page Breaks—Manual—Adding 133
Page Breaks—Manual—Deleting 134
Printing—Document 135
Printing—Page Setup 137
Printing—Print Preview 140
Printing—Removing Print Area 141
Printing—Removing Print Titles 142
Printing—Setting Print Area 143
Printing—Setting Print Titles 143

Range—Applying Names 144
Range—Defining Names 146
Range—Deleting Names 147
Range—Editing Names 148
Range—Filling Cells Down 149
Range—Filling Cells Right 150
Range—Filling with Series 152

Repeating—Operations and Commands 155
Row—Changing Height 156
Row—Deleting 157
Row—Inserting 157

Selecting Cells 157
Selecting—Multiple Ranges of Cells 159
Selecting—Special Data 159
Shortcut Menu 161
Spelling—Checking 161

Toolbars—Selecting Tool 164
Toolbar—Showing and Hiding 165
Toolbar—Tool Description 165

Undo—Commands and Operations 166

Window—Activating 167
Window—Arranging 168
Window—Arranging Icons 169
Window—Closing Window 169
Window—Freezing and Unfreezing 170
Window—Hiding and Unhiding 171
Window—Maximizing Window 172
Window—Minimizing Window 173
Window—Moving Window 174
Window—New Window 175
Window—Next Window 175
Window—Restoring Window 176
Window—Sizing Window 176
Window—Splitting Window 177
Window—Zooming 178
Workbook—Adding Existing Documents 180
Workbook—Adding New Documents 181
Workbook—Creating 182
Workbook—Opening a Document 183
Workbook—Removing Documents 184
Workbook—Saving 185
Worksheet—Grouping and Ungrouping 186
Workspace—Setting Options 187

Common Excel Functions 191
Index 195

Introduction

With short and clear step-by-step instructions, the *One Minute Reference Excel 4* offers unique help when you are in a hurry. This book is designed for the person who:

- Doesn't have time to flip through a large manual.

- Only wants the necessary steps to accomplish a task and not a lot of text.

- Wants no-nonsense instructions to complete a task.

The *One Minute Reference Excel 4* explains the tasks you need to accomplish in easy-to-understand, quick steps.

Conventions Used in This Book

This book presents Excel in ways that will make using the program as simple as possible:

- Excel tasks are organized in alphabetical order for instant fingertip access to important topics.

- All steps are concise; listed to the right of each step you will find the keys you need to press (or information you need to type) to accomplish a task.

- Keys to press are shown as
  keycaps, like this .... ⏎

- Information to type is shown in
  bold italic text, like this ....***text***

- **(Optional)** Some steps may begin with this notation. Bypass the step if you do not want to use the option.

- **Ctrl+** or **Alt+** These are key combinations used to accomplish an Excel task. For example, if you are asked to press **Alt+A**, press the **Alt** key and the **A** at the same time.

- **OR** If you see an "OR" in a step, you can choose another specified way to follow the step.

- When a step takes more than one keypress or action, you'll see them listed vertically. ....

This icon points out additional information and techniques you may find valuable as you use Excel 4.0's features.

This icon gives examples of how to use the feature being discussed, for better understanding.

One Minute Reference Excel 4

Trademarks

All terms mentioned in this book that are known to be trademarks have been appropriately capitalized. Alpha Books cannot attest to the accuracy of this information. Use of a term in this book should not be regarded as affecting the validity of any trademark or service mark.

Microsoft Excel Basics

Microsoft Excel is a powerful spreadsheet program and more. Excel performs calculations and analyses (including the "what-if" type) on worksheets. It also outlines worksheets, formats data, automates routine tasks with macros, and offers database, charting and drawing features. Before you can take advantage of Excel, however, you must learn some Excel basics.

Starting Microsoft Excel

To start Excel, do the following:

1. At the DOS prompt, type ....**win**

2. Press .... ⏎

3. Once you see the Windows Desktop (the background) and the Program Manager (which lets you organize and start programs), open the program group that contains the Microsoft Excel icon.

4. Double-click on the **Microsoft Excel** icon, or highlight the icon and press **Enter**.

The Excel title screen appears for a few moments. Then an empty worksheet will appear; you can begin working on it right away (see Figure 1).

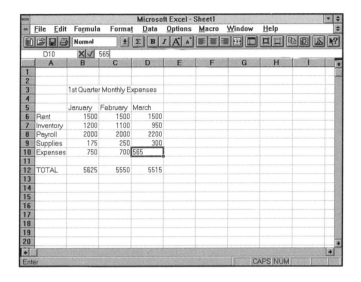

Figure 1   The Excel worksheet screen.

Parts of an Excel Screen

The Excel screen contains elements you won't see in DOS. Here's a brief summary:

- **Title bar**   Located along the top of a window or screen; shows the name of the window or program.

- **Cell**   A single box where text and numerical data is entered.

- **Active Cell**   The cell which is selected and where any changes will be made. Each cell

Microsoft Excel Basics

has an **address** that consists of its column letter and row number. For example, the cell in row 2 of column B is cell **B2**. Cell **ranges** (contiguous groups of cells) are identified by the address of the upper left cell and the lower right cell, separated by a colon, as in **A1:B5**.

- **Row**   The horizontal cells in the worksheet.

- **Column**   The vertical cells in the worksheet.

- **Reference Area**   Displays the address for the active cell.

- **Cancel Box**   Click to cancel the entry in the active cell.

- **Enter Box**   Click to accept the entry in the active cell.

- **Toolbar**   Contains the tools that perform common Excel commands and functions.

- **Tools**   Graphic representations of Excel commands. To use a tool, you click on the tool in the toolbar.

- **Minimize and Maximize buttons**   Located at the upper right corner of a window or screen, these look like a down arrow and an up arrow. They alter a window's size. The Minimize button shrinks the window to the size of an icon. The Maximize button expands the window to fill the screen. When maximized, a window contains a double-arrow **Restore** button, which returns the window to its original size.

- **Control menu box**   Located in the upper left corner of a window or screen; looks like a box with a hyphen in it. When selected, pulls down a menu that offers size and location controls for the window.

- **Pull-down menu bar**   Located below the title bar, this contains a list of the pull-down menus available in Excel.

- **Mouse Pointer**   If you are using a mouse, the mouse pointer (usually an arrow) appears on-screen. It can be controlled by moving the mouse.

- **Scroll bars**   If a window contains more information than can be displayed in the window, a scroll bar appears; usually located at the bottom or right side of a window, or both. **Scroll arrows** on each end of the scroll bar allow you to scroll slowly. The **scroll box** allows you to scroll more quickly.

Microsoft Excel Basics

Using a Mouse

To work most efficiently in Excel, you should use a mouse. You can press mouse buttons and move the mouse in various ways to change the way it acts:

- **Point** means to move the mouse pointer onto the specified item by moving the mouse. The tip of the mouse pointer must be touching the item.

- **Click** on an item means to move the pointer onto the specified item, and then press the mouse button once. Unless specified otherwise, use the left mouse button.

- **Double-click** on an item means to move the pointer onto the specified item, and then press and release the mouse button twice quickly.

- **Drag** means to move the mouse pointer onto the specified item, hold down the mouse button, and move the mouse while holding down the button.

Choosing Menus and Commands

*The pull-down menu bar contains various menus from which you can select commands. Each menu name, and the commands on the menu, have an underlined letter. This is the **selection letter** that* *you can use to choose the menu or command with the keyboard. (Selection letters are indicated in* **bold** *in this book.) To open a menu and choose a command, use the steps described next.*

Keyboard Steps

1. Choose the menu .... Alt + *selection letter*
2. Choose the command .... *selection letter*

Mouse Steps

1. Click on the menu name on the menu bar.
2. Click on the desired command.

TIP

*Notice that some commands are followed by key names such as **F12** or **Alt+F4**. These are called **accelerator keys**. You can use these keys to perform these commands without even opening the menu.*

Usually, when you select a command, the command is performed immediately. However:

- If the command name is **gray** (rather than black), the command is unavailable at the moment and you cannot choose it.

- If the command name is followed by an **arrow**, selecting the command will cause another menu to appear, from which you select another command.

Microsoft Excel Basics

- If the command name is followed by **ellipses** (three dots), selecting it will cause a dialog box to appear. You'll learn about dialog boxes in the next section.

Navigating Dialog Boxes

*A **dialog box** is Excel's way of requesting additional information. Each dialog box contains one or more of the following elements:*

- **List boxes** display available choices. To activate a list, click inside the list box. If the entire list is not visible, use the scroll bar to view the items in the list. To select an item from the list, click on it.

- **Drop-down lists** are similar to list boxes, but only one item in the list is shown. To see the rest of the items, click on the down arrow to the right of the list box. To select an item from the list, click on it.

- **Text boxes** allow you to type an entry. To activate a text box, click inside it. To edit an existing entry, use the arrow keys to move the cursor, and the Del or Backspace keys to delete existing characters, and then type your correction.

- **Check boxes** allow you to select one or more items in a group of options. For example, if you are styling text, you may select Bold and Italic to have the text appear in both bold and italic type. Click on a check box to activate it.

- **Option buttons** are like check boxes, but you can select only one option button in a group. Selecting one button deselects any option that is already selected. Click on an option button to activate it.

- **Command buttons** execute (or cancel) the command once you have made your selections in the dialog box. To press a command button, click on it.

Using the Keyboard

Press	Description
Tab	Moves forward through the dialog box.
Shift + Tab	Moves backwards through the dialog box.
Alt + *selection letter*	Moves directly to the option.

continues

continued

Press	Description
↑ or ↓	Moves through a list box.
Page Up or Page Down	Moves through a list box.
Space	Turn active check box off and on.
↵	Selects the OK button.
Esc	Selects the Cancel button.

Cell—Adding Borders

Adds a border and shading around selected cells.

Keyboard Steps

1. Select the cells (see **Selecting Cells**) to surround with a border.

   TIP *To select the entire worksheet to surround with a border, press* ***Ctrl+Shift+Spacebar***.

2. Select the Forma**t** menu .... `Alt` + `T`
3. Select **B**order .... `B`
4. Select any of the following options:
   Outline .... `Alt` + `O`
   Left .... `Alt` + `L`
   Right .... `Alt` + `R`
   Top .... `Alt` + `T`
   Bottom .... `Alt` + `B`
   Sty**l**e .... `Alt` + `E`
   Color .... `Alt` + `C`
   Shade .... `Alt` + `S`
5. When finished adding border, press .... `↵`

Mouse Steps

1. Select the cells (see **Selecting Cells**) to surround with a border.

*You can also select **Border** from the shortcut menu. To display the shortcut menu, point to the selected cells and click the right mouse button.*

2. Click on the Format menu.

3. Click on **Border**.

4. Click any of the following options:
    Outline
    Left
    Right
    Top
    Bottom
    St**y**le
    Color
    Shade

5. When finished adding the border, click on **OK**.

*To add borders to selected cells, click on the **Outline** and **Bottom Border** tools from the **Standard** toolbar, and the **Top Border** and **Left Border** tools from the **Custom** toolbar.*

Cell—Deleting

Deletes a selected cell, row, or column (including data, formulas, and formatting) from the active worksheet. The cells surrounding the deletion will shift to fill the empty space.

There may be confusion between the Edit Clear and Edit Delete command. Edit Clear simply removes the contents of a cell. Edit Delete removes the cell itself, shifting cells to eliminate the deleted cell.

Keyboard Steps

1. Select the cell, row, or column to Delete (see **Selecting Cells**).
2. To select the Edit menu, press .... Alt + E
3. Select Delete .... D

*You can also press **Ctrl+−** (minus sign) to delete selected cells, rows, or columns.*

Cell—Deleting

4. Select any of the following options from the Delete dialog box:
   Shift Cells **L**eft .... Alt + L
   Shift Cells **U**p .... Alt + U
   Entire **R**ow .... Alt + R
   Entire **C**olumn .... Alt + C

5. When ready to Delete the selection, press .... ↵

Mouse Steps

1. Click on the cell(s), row, or column you want to delete.

To select an entire row or column, click on the row or column head.

2. Click on the **E**dit menu.
3. Click on **D**elete.

*In place of steps 2 and 3, you can click the right mouse button to bring up the shortcut menu, and select **Delete**.*

4. Click on any of the following options from the Delete dialog box:
   Shift Cells **L**eft
   Shift Cells **U**p
   Entire **R**ow
   Entire **C**olumn

Cell—Deleting

5. When ready to delete the selection, click on **OK**.

Cell—Goto

Searches a document, going directly to the cell, range of cells, or named range you specify.

EXAMPLE

You can use this command when you have large worksheets and don't want to use your scroll keys to look for your selection. You can jump across large numbers of cells. For example, if you are presently in cell C10 and want to go to a cell several screens away (like AZ355), you can use the Goto command.

Keyboard Steps

1. Select the Formula menu .... **Alt** + **R**
2. Select Goto .... **G**

*Pressing **F5** also lets you go to a specified cell.*

TIP

3. In the Reference box, enter a cell's address, range, or range name to go to .... **Alt** + **R**

4. When ready to go to the
   cell(s), press .... ⏎

Mouse Steps

1. Click on the Formula menu.
2. Click on Goto.
3. In the Reference box, enter a cell's address, range, or range name to go to.
4. When ready to go to the chosen cell(s), click on **OK**.

Cell—Inserting

Inserts a blank cell, range, row, or column into the active worksheet. The inserted cells appear in whatever location and shape you select. Inserting will shift the cells surrounding the insertion to make room.

Keyboard Steps

1. Select a cell, range, row, or column insert (see **Selecting Cells**).
2. Select the Edit menu .... Alt + E
3. Select Insert I

Cell—Goto

TIP *You can also press **Ctrl**+ **+** (plus sign) to display the dialog box that lets you insert selected cells, rows, or columns. You can use the **+** on the numeric keypad, or hold down* **Ctrl**+**Shift**, *then press the* **+** *key on the regular keyboard.*

4. Select any of the following options from the Insert dialog box:
   Shift Cells Right .... `Alt` + `I`
   Shift Cells Down .... `Alt` + `D`
   Entire Row .... `Alt` + `R`
   Entire Column .... `Alt` + `C`

5. When ready to insert the selection, press ....

Mouse Steps

1. Select the cell(s), range, row, or column you want to insert (see **Selecting Cells**).

TIP *To select an entire row or column, click on the row or column head.*

2. Click on the Edit menu.
3. Click on Insert.

Cell—Inserting

*In place of steps 2 and 3, you can click the right mouse button to bring up the shortcut menu, and select **Insert**.*

4. Click on any of the following options from the Insert dialog box:
   Shift Cells **R**ight
   Shift Cells **D**own
   Entire **R**ow
   Entire **C**olumn

5. When ready to insert the selection, click on **OK**.

*Click on any of the **Insert** tools found in the **Custom** toolbar to insert blank cells, rows, or columns into a worksheet.*

Cell—Selecting

*See **Selecting Cells** for information on selecting cells, rows, columns, and ranges.*

Cell—Showing Active Cell

Searches the worksheet to find and display the active cell.

Keyboard Steps

1. Select the Formula menu .... [Alt] + [R]
2. Select Show Active Cell .... [H]

Mouse Steps

1. Click on the Formula menu.
2. Click on Show Active Cell.

Cell Notes—Adding

Allows you to attach notes to a cell, and places a note indicator in the upper right corner of the cell. Attaching cell notes can remind you (and others using your spreadsheets) of important information in the cell, or how the information was calculated or gathered.

EXAMPLE

You can use this feature, for example, to add a note to a cell with a formula, describing how you came up with formula. For example, your note in a cell with a formula could be "This formula calculates net profit by subtracting expenses in cell D50 from income in cell G72."

TIP *If you do not see the note indicator in the cell with the note (or would like to turn off the indicator), select the Options menu by pressing Alt+O or clicking on it. Then choose Workspace by pressing Alt+W or clicking on it. Turn the Note Indicator check box on or off by pressing Alt+N or clicking, and then press Enter or click on OK.*

Keyboard Steps

1. Select the cell you want to attach a cell note to (see **Selecting Cells**).

2. Select the Formula menu .... `Alt` + `R`

3. Select Note .... `N`

4. In the Text Note box, add the cell note .... `Alt` + `T`
   text

5. **(Optional)** To add another cell note, select Add .... `Alt` + `A`

6. When finished attaching a cell note, press .... `↵`

Mouse Steps

1. Click on the cell you want to attach a cell note to (see **Selecting Cells**).

2. Click on the Formula menu.

10 Cell Notes—Adding

3. Click on **Note**.

4. In the **T**ext Note box, enter or edit a cell note.

5. **(Optional)** Click on the **A**dd button to add more cell notes.

6. When finished attaching the cell note(s), click on **OK**.

Cell Notes—Viewing, Editing or Deleting

You can view, edit, or delete notes attached to a cell.

Keyboard Steps

1. Select the cell with the note (look for the note indicator in the upper right corner).

2. Select the Formula menu .... **Alt** + **R**

3. Select Note .... **N**

*For a quick display of the cell note for the selected cell, press **Shift+F2**.*

4. In the **T**ext Note box, view or edit the cell note .... **Alt** + **T**

Cell Notes—Viewing, Editing or Deleting

TIP

*To delete a cell note, go to the Notes in Sheet box by pressing **Alt+S**, and select a note by using ↑ or ↓. Then select the **Delete** button by pressing **Alt+D**.*

5. When finished editing a cell note, press ....

Mouse Steps

1. Double-click on the cell with the note (look for the note indicator in the upper right corner of the cell).

2. In the Text Note box, view or edit the cell note.

TIP

*To delete a cell note, click on a note in the Notes in Sheet box, and click on the **Delete** button.*

3. When finished viewing or editing cell notes, click on **OK**.

Chart—Activating

Makes the selected chart the active chart so you can edit, format, and add arrows, text, colors, etc.

- To activate an embedded chart, double-click anywhere on the chart.

- To activate a chart which has been created in its own window, select File ....`Alt` + `F`
  Select Open ....`O`
  Select the chart file by typing the file name ....*filename*
  Click on **OK** or press ....`↵`

Chart—Arrow—Adding

Adds an arrow to the active chart.

Keyboard Steps

1. If it is not already active, activate the chart to which you are adding an arrow (see **Chart—Activating**).

2. Select the Chart menu ....`Alt` + `C`

3. Select Add Arrow ....`R`

4. **(Optional)** To reposition the arrow, select the Forma**t** menu ....`Alt` + `T`
   Select Move ....`V`
   Move the arrow as desired ....`↑` `↓` `←` `→`
   Press ....`↵`

Chart—Arrow—Adding 13

Mouse Steps

1. Activate the chart to which you are adding an arrow by double-clicking on the chart (see **Chart—Activating**).
2. Click on the Chart menu.
3. Click on Add Arrow.
4. **(Optional)** To move the arrow, click on the Format menu.
   Click on Move.
   Drag the arrow to the desired location.

*Click on the **Arrow** tool on the **Chart** toolbar to add an arrow to the active chart.*

Chart—Arrow—Deleting

Deletes an arrow from the active chart.

Keyboard Steps

1. In the active chart, select the arrow to delete .... [↑] [↓] [←] [→]
2. Select the Chart menu .... [Alt] + [C]
3. Select Delete Arrow .... [R]

*You can also delete an arrow by selecting the arrow you want to delete, and pressing the **Del** key.*

Mouse Steps

1. Click on the arrow you want to delete from the active chart.
2. Click on the Chart menu.
3. Click on Delete Arrow.

Chart—Attaching Text

Adds text to a chart which you specify.

Keyboard Steps

1. Activate the chart if it is not already active (see **Chart—Activating**).
2. Select the Chart menu .... `Alt` + `C`
3. Select Attach Text .... `T`
4. Select an option from the Attach Text To box .... `Tab` or `↑` or `↓`
5. Press .... `↵`
6. Type the text to add in the formula bar .... ***text***

7. Press .... ⏎

Mouse Steps

1. Activate the chart if it is not already active by double-clicking on it.
2. Click on the Chart menu.
3. Click on Attach Text.
4. Click on an option in the Attach Text To box.
5. Click on **OK**.
6. Type the text to add in the formula bar.
7. Click on **OK**.

*Click on the **Text** tool in the **Chart** toolbar to attach text to a chart.*

Chart—Axes

*Displays or hides the X- and Y-axes' labels and markers. **Axis labels** are the text along the X and Y axes that describes the chart data.*

Keyboard Steps

1. Activate the chart if it is not already active (see **Chart—Activating**).

2. Select the Chart menu .... `Alt` + `C`

3. Select Axes .... `X`

4. Select the axes to display or hide. Clearing the check box hides the axes .... `↑` or `↓`

5. Press .... `↵`

Mouse Steps

1. Activate the chart (if it is not already active) by double-clicking on it.

2. Click on the Chart menu.

3. Click on Chart Axes.

4. Click on the axes to display or hide. Clearing the check box hides the axes.

5. Click on **OK**.

Chart—Calculate Now

*Recalculates the formulas in all open worksheets and updates the corresponding charts. You need perform this operation only if you have set your formulas to calculate manually (see **Formula— Setting Calculation Options**).*

Keyboard Steps

1. Activate the chart if it is not already active (see **Chart—Activating**).

2. Select the Chart menu .... Alt + C
3. Select Calculate Now .... N

Press F9 to calculate quickly.

Mouse Steps

1. Activate the chart (if it is not already active) by double-clicking on it.
2. Click on the Chart menu.
3. Click on Calculate Now.

*Click on the **Calculate** tool from the **Utility** toolbar to recalculate all open worksheets.*

Chart—Color Palette—Changing

*Changes the colors in the color palette for the active chart. (To change the colors on other charts, see **Chart—Color Palette—Copying**. Note: this option cannot be used with embedded charts; it will be dimmed on the Chart menu.)*

Keyboard Steps

1. Activate the chart if it is not already active (see **Chart —Activating**).
2. Select the Chart menu .... `Alt` + `C`
3. Select Color Palette .... `E`
4. Select a color to change .... `↑` or `↓`
5. Select the Edit button .... `Alt` + `E`
6. Select a replacement color .... `↑` or `↓`

You can adjust the Hue, Sat (saturation), Lum (luminosity), and Red, Green, and Blue color tones of the color you are changing.

To reset the colors to their original defaults, select the Default button by pressing Alt+D.

7. Press .... `↵`

Mouse Steps

1. Activate the chart (if it is not already active) by double-clicking on it.
2. Click on the Chart menu.

Chart—Color Palette—Changing

3. Click on Color Palette.
4. Click on a color to change.
5. Click on the Edit button.
6. Click on a color to replace the color in the palette.

You can adjust the Hue, Sat (saturation), Lum (luminosity), and Red, Green, and Blue color tones of the color you are changing.

7. Click on **OK**.

To reset the colors to their original defaults, click on the Default button.

Chart—Creating with ChartWizard

ChartWizard leads you through the creation of an embedded chart step-by-step. (Note: you can only use ChartWizard with a mouse.)

*An **embedded chart** sits on top of your worksheet (not in its own file), and can be edited, moved, sized, and formatted.*

Mouse Steps

1. Click on the ChartWizard tool on the Standard toolbar.
2. Select the range of cells on the worksheet containing the data you want to chart.
3. Click on **Next** or press **Enter**.
4. Click on a chart type.
5. Click on **Next** or press **Enter**.
6. Click on a chart format.
7. Click on **Next** or press **Enter**.
8. Click on any of the layout options.
9. Click on **Next** or press **Enter**.
10. Click on any text options.
11. Click on **OK** or press **Enter**.

Chart—Creating with Toolbar

Creates a predefined embedded chart in a worksheet by selecting a charting tool from the Chart toolbar.

*An **embedded chart** sits on top of your worksheet (not in its own file), and can be edited, moved, sized, and formatted.*

Mouse Steps

1. Select the cell range with the data you want to chart.
2. Click on a charting tool from the Chart toolbar.
3. Click on the upper left corner of the area you want as the chart area.
4. Drag to the lower right corner of the chart area, and release the mouse button.

Chart—Creating in Separate Document

Creates a chart in a separate document from the data.

EXAMPLE *If you create a chart in a separate document, you could use the Copy, Cut, and Paste commands to paste the chart into other documents. For example, if you created a chart depicting your expenses compared to your income, you could paste the chart into your expense document, balance sheet document, annual report, etc.*

Keyboard Steps

1. Select the cell range which contains the data you want to chart (see **Selecting Cells**).
2. Select the File menu .... Alt + F
3. Select New .... N

To create a chart quickly in a separate document, press F11 or Alt+F1.

4. Highlight the Chart option .... ↑ or ↓
5. To create the chart, press .... ↵

Mouse Steps

1. Select the cell range which contains the data you want to chart (see **Selecting Cells**).
2. Click on the File menu.
3. Click on **New**.
4. Click on the Chart option.
5. To create the chart, click on **OK**.

Chart—Creating in Separate Document

Chart—Editing Series

Edits or creates a data series in the active chart.

Keyboard Steps

1. Activate the chart if it is not already active (see **Chart —Activating**).

2. Select the Chart menu .... **Alt** + **C**

3. Select Edit Series .... **I**

4. Select a series to edit
   in the Series box .... **↑** or **↓**
   Press .... **Tab**

   OR

   Select a new series to add .... **↑** or **↓**
   Press .... **Tab**

5. **(Optional)** Edit the formulas in the **Name**, **X** Labels, **Y** Values, or **Z** Values text boxes.

6. **(Optional)** Define the plot order for the data series by typing an order number in the **Plot** Order box .... **Alt** + **P**
   order number

7. Press .... ⏎

Mouse Steps

1. Activate the chart (if it is not already active) by double-clicking on it.

2. Click on the **Chart** menu.

3. Click on Edit Series.

*In place of steps 2 and 3, you can click the right mouse button to bring up the shortcut menu, and select **Edit Series**.*

4. Click on a series to edit in the **Series** box.

   OR

   Click on New Series to add a series.

5. **(Optional)** Edit the formulas in the **Name**, **X** Labels, **Y** Values, or **Z** Values boxes.

6. **(Optional)** Define the plot order for the data series by clicking in the **P**lot Order box and typing an order number.

7. Click on **OK**.

Chart—Editing Series

Chart—Formatting 3-D View

Formats the angle in which the 3-D chart is viewed.

Keyboard Steps

1. Activate the chart if it is not already active (see **Chart—Activating**).

2. Select the Format menu .... **Alt** + **T**

3. Select 3-D View **3**

4. Make any necessary changes to the Elevation, Rotation, and Right Angle Axes.

5. Select Apply after changing the settings .... **Alt** + **A**

> *To reset the settings, select Default by pressing Alt+D.*

6. Press .... **↵**

Mouse Steps

1. Activate the chart (if it is not already active) by double-clicking on it.

2. Click on the Format menu.

3. Click on **3**-D View.
4. Make any necessary changes to the Elevation, Rotation, and Right Angle Axes.
5. Click on **A**pply after changing the settings.
6. Click on **OK**.

To reset the settings, click on Default.

Chart—Formatting Main Chart

Enables you to change the chart type without changing the chart formatting for the active chart.

Keyboard Steps

1. Activate the chart if it is not already active (see **Chart —Activating**).
2. Select the Forma**t** menu .... **Alt** + **T**
3. Select **M**ain Chart .... **M**
4. Select a chart type from the Main Chart **T**ype list box .... **Alt** + **T**
   Select chart type .... **↑** or **↓**
   Area
   Bar

Column
Line
Pie
XY (Scatter)
Radar
3-D Area
3-D Bar
3-D Column
3-D Line
3-D Pie
3-D Surface

5. Change any of the following formatting options (these may vary depending on the chart type):

Data View	Alt + I
Overlap	Alt + O
Gap Width	Alt + W
Series Lines	Alt + S
Vary by Category	Alt + V
Drop Lines	Alt + D
Hi-Lo Lines	Alt + L
Up/Down Bars	Alt + U
Radar Axis Labels	Alt + R
Angle of First Pie Slice	Alt + E
3-D Gap Depth	Alt + G
3-D Chart Depth	Alt + C

6. To apply the settings, press ....

Mouse Steps

1. Activate the chart (if it is not already active) by double-clicking on it.
2. Click on the Format menu.
3. Click on Main Chart.

In place of steps 2 and 3, you can click the right mouse button to bring up the shortcut menu, and select Main Chart.

4. Click on the Main Chart Type list box.
5. Click on one of the following chart types:
   Area
   Bar
   Column
   Line
   Pie
   XY (Scatter)
   Radar
   3-D Area
   3-D Bar
   3-D Column
   3-D Line
   3-D Pie
   3-D Surface

6. Change any of the following formatting options by clicking on them (options may vary depending on the chart type):
   Data **V**iew
   Overlap
   Gap **W**idth
   Series Lines
   Vary by Category
   Drop Lines
   Hi-Lo Lines
   Up/Down Bars
   Radar Axis Labels
   An**g**le of First Pie Slice
   3-D **G**ap Depth
   3-D **C**hart Depth

7. To apply the settings, click on **OK**.

Chart—Gallery

Provides a list of predefined chart types to choose from. (Note: choosing a predefined chart type changes the chart type of the active chart.)

Keyboard Steps

1. Activate the chart if it is not already active (see **Chart—Activating**).

2. Select **Gallery** from the menu .... `Alt` + `G`
3. Select a chart type .... `↑` or `↓`
4. Press .... `↵`
5. Select a predefined chart type to apply to the active chart .... `←` or `→`

TIP

You can select the Next or Previous buttons to change the chart type by pressing Alt+N or Alt+P.

6. To apply the predefined format, press .... `↵`

Mouse Steps

1. Activate the chart (if it is not already active) by double-clicking on it.
2. Click on the **Gallery** menu.
3. Click on a chart type.
4. Double-click on a predefined chart format.

TIP

Click on the Next and Previous buttons to change the chart type.

Chart—Gallery

*You can click on any charting tool from the **Chart** toolbar to change the active chart.*

TIP

Chart—Gridlines

Displays or hides the Major and Minor gridlines on the active chart.

Keyboard Steps

1. Activate the chart if it is not already active (see **Chart —Activating**).
2. Select the Chart menu .... `Alt` + `C`
3. Select Gridlines .... `G`
4. In the **Category (X) axis** box, select Major Gridlines, Minor Gridlines, or both .... `Alt` + `M` or `Alt` + `I`
5. In the **Value (Y) axis** box, select Major Gridlines, Minor Gridlines, or both .... `Alt` + `O` or `Alt` + `N`
6. Press .... `↵`

Mouse Steps

1. Activate the chart if it is not already active (see **Chart—Activating**).
2. Click on the Chart menu.
3. Click on Gridlines.

*In place of steps 2 and 3, you can click the right mouse button to bring up the shortcut menu, and select **Gridlines**.*

4. In the **Category (X) axis** box, click on Major Gridlines, Minor Gridlines, or both.
5. In the **Value (Y) axis** box, click Major Gridlines, Minor Gridlines, or both.
6. Click on **OK**.

*To add gridlines to a chart, you can click on the **Horizontal Gridlines** tool from the **Chart** toolbar, or the **Vertical Gridlines** tool (this is custom tool that can be added to a toolbar).*

Chart—Legend—Adding

Adds a legend to the active chart.

*A **legend** is simply a box where the data series in the chart are identified.*

Keyboard Steps

1. Activate the chart if it is not already active (see **Chart—Activating**).

2. Select the Chart menu .... `Alt` + `C`

3. Select Add Legend .... `L`

4. **(Optional)** To reposition the legend, select Format .... `Alt` + `T`

   Select Move .... `V`

   Move the legend to the desired location .... `↑` `↓` `←` `→`

Mouse Steps

1. Activate the chart if it is not already active (see **Chart—Activating**).

2. Click on the Chart menu.

3. Click on Add Legend.

4. **(Optional)** To reposition the legend, click on the legend and drag it to the desired position.

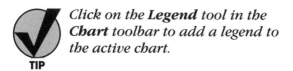

*Click on the **Legend** tool in the **Chart** toolbar to add a legend to the active chart.*

Chart—Legend—Deleting

Deletes the legend from the active chart.

Keyboard Steps

1. Activate the chart if it is not already active (see **Chart—Activating**).

2. Select the legend to delete from the chart .... ↑ ↓ ← →

3. Select the Chart menu .... Alt + C

4. Select Delete Legend L

*You can also delete the legend by selecting it and pressing the **Del** key.*

Mouse Steps

1. Activate the chart (if it is not already active) by double-clicking on it.

2. Click on the legend to delete.
3. Click on the Chart menu.
4. Click on Delete Legend.

Chart—Moving and Sizing Embedded

Moves or sizes the embedded chart in the document. (You may need to do so to keep the chart from hiding your worksheet information. Note that you must use a mouse for this procedure.)

Mouse Steps

1. Click anywhere on the chart. Black selection handles will appear around the chart.
2. If you wish to move the chart, drag it to the desired location.
3. If you wish to size the chart, point to any of the selection handles, press and hold the left mouse button, and drag to the desired size.

Chart—Moving Object

Allows you to move the objects on a chart.

Keyboard Steps

1. Activate the chart if it is not already active (see **Chart —Activating**).

2. Select the chart object
   to move .... `↑` `↓` `←` `→`
3. Select the Format menu .... `Alt` + `T`
4. Select Move .... `V`
5. Move the object to
   its new location .... `↑` `↓` `←` `→`
6. When the object is in
   the desired location, press .... `↵`

Mouse Steps

1. Activate the chart (if it is not already active) by double-clicking on it.
2. Click on the chart object to move.
3. Drag the object to its new location.

Chart—Overlay—Adding

*Creates an overlay (second chart) over the active chart. Adding an overlay chart creates a **combination chart**.*

Keyboard Steps

1. Activate the chart if it is not already active (see **Chart—Activating**).
2. Select the Chart menu .... `Alt` + `C`

3. Select Add Overlay .... `O`

4. **(Optional)** To format the overlay chart, select the Format menu .... `Alt` + `T`

   Select Overlay .... `O`

Mouse Steps

1. Activate the chart (if it is not already active) by double-clicking on it.

2. Click on the Chart menu.

3. Click on Add Overlay.

4. **(Optional)** To format the overlay chart, click on the Format menu, and then click on Overlay.

Chart—Overlay—Deleting

Deletes the overlay chart.

Keyboard Steps

1. Activate the chart if it is not already active (see **Chart—Activating**).

2. Select the Chart menu .... `Alt` + `C`

3. Select Delete Overlay .... `O`

38 Chart—Overlay—Adding

Mouse Steps

1. Activate the chart (if it is not already active) by double-clicking on it.
2. Click on the Chart menu.
3. Click on Delete Overlay.

Chart—Protecting Documents

Protects a chart from changes being made to either the data or the formatting, and allows you to add a password. (Note: you cannot protect an embedded chart.)

Keyboard Steps

1. Activate the chart if it is not already active (see **Chart—Activating**).
2. Select the Chart menu .... `Alt` + `C`
3. Select Protect Document .... `P`
4. **(Optional)** If the Chart check box is not checked, select it .... `Alt` + `C`
5. **(Optional)** Enter a password in the Password text box .... `Alt` + `P`

   Type a password ....*password*

6. **(Optional)** To prevent formatting changes, check the **W**indows check box .... `Alt` + `W`

7. Press .... `↵`

Mouse Steps

1. Activate the chart (if it is not already active) by double-clicking on it.

2. Click on the **C**hart menu.

3. Click on **P**rotect Document.

4. **(Optional)** If the **C**hart check box is not checked, click on it.

5. **(Optional)** Click on the **P**assword text box and enter a password.

6. **(Optional)** To prevent changes to the formatting, check the **W**indows check box.

7. Click on **OK**.

Chart—Scaling

Enables the changing of the scale settings for each chart axis.

EXAMPLE *Changing the scaling of a chart makes a big difference in impact. By reducing or enlarging the values of the axis, you can make the chart clearer and more concise, bringing dramatic emphasis to the data.*

Keyboard Steps

1. Activate the chart if it is not already active (see **Chart—Activating**).

2. Select an axis on the active chart .... ↑ ↓ ← →

3. Select the Format menu .... Alt + T

4. Select Scale .... S

5. Change any scaling option for the selected axis by pressing .... Alt + *selection letter*

6. To accept the scaling settings, press .... ⏎

Mouse Steps

1. Activate the chart (if it is not already active) by double-clicking on it.

2. Click on one of the axes on the active chart.

3. Click on the Format menu.

4. Change any of the scaling options for the selected axis.

5. To accept the scaling settings, click on **OK**.

Chart—Selecting Entire

Selects all the elements in the active chart (including its labels, legends, arrows, and attached text) so you can edit or format the entire chart.

Keyboard Steps

1. Activate the chart if it is not already active (see **Chart —Activating**).
2. Select the Chart menu .... **Alt** + **C**
3. Select Select Chart .... **C**
4. Edit or apply formatting to the selected chart as desired.

*TIP — To deselect a selected chart, simply press **Esc**. Deselecting a chart does not close the chart window. It no longer makes the chart window active.*

Mouse Steps

1. Activate the chart (if it is not already active) by double-clicking on it.
2. Click on the Chart menu.

3. Click on Select Chart.
4. Edit or apply formatting to the selected chart as desired.

To select the entire chart quickly, click outside the plot area of the chart.

Chart—Sizing Objects

Allows the sizing of objects (arrows and unattached text) on the active chart.

1. Activate the chart if it is not already active (see **Chart —Activating**).
2. In the active chart, select the object you want to size.
3. Select the Format menu .... **Alt** + **T**
4. Select Size .... **Z**
5. Size the object, using .... **↑** **↓** **←** **→**

*To size the object in smaller increments, press the **Ctrl** key while pressing the **arrow** keys.*

6. When finished sizing the
object, press .... ⏎

Mouse Steps

1. Activate the chart (if it is not already active) by double-clicking on it.

2. In the active chart, click on the object you want to size.

3. Click and drag the selection handles (black squares) to size the object.

Chart—Unprotecting

Unprotects the active protected chart which has been given a password.

Keyboard Steps

1. Activate the chart if it is not already active (see **Chart —Activating**).

2. Select the Chart menu .... Alt + C

3. Select Unprotect Document .... P

4. Enter the password .... ***password***

5. Press .... ⏎

Mouse Steps

1. Activate the chart (if it is not already active) by double-clicking on it.

2. Click on the **Chart** menu.
3. Click on Unprotect Document.
4. Enter the password.
5. Click on **OK**.

Column—Changing Width

*Changes the width of the column to accommodate larger amounts of data. (See **Selecting Cells** for more information on how to select cells, columns, rows, and ranges.)*

If you make the column too small to display the contents of a cell, you will see pound signs (####) in the cell.

Keyboard Steps

1. Select a cell from each column or a range of columns whose width you want to change.

*You can change the column widths of the entire worksheet by pressing **Shift+Spacebar** to select an entire row, then changing column width.*

2. Select the Format menu .... **Alt** + **T**

3. Select **C**olumn Width C

4. In the Column Width box, enter the number of characters (0–255) you want to fit in the cell .... ***number***

5. **(Optional)** Select the **B**est Fit button for automatic adjustment based on cell contents .... Alt + B

TIP: To reset the column back to the standard width, check the Use Standard Width check box by pressing Alt+S.

6. **(Optional)** You can select the **H**ide command to set the width to 0 and hide the column .... Alt + H

7. When finished setting column width, press .... ⏎

Mouse Steps

1. Click on a column heading.
2. Drag the right border to adjust the size.

Column—Changing Width

To adjust the width for multiple columns, drag across the column letters to highlight (select) the columns. Then use the Format Column Width command as described for the preceding Keyboard Steps.

Column—Deleting

See Cell—Deleting

Column-Inserting

See Cell—Inserting

Data—Aligning Data

Aligns the data within selected cells. The following table lists the options found in the Alignment dialog box.

Options	Description
Horizontal	
General	Left-aligns text and right-aligns numbers (this is the default alignment).
Left	Left-aligns data.
Center	Centers data.
Right	Right-aligns data.
Fill	Repeats a character to fill a cell.

continues

Data—Aligning Data 47

continued

Options	Description
Justify	Aligns text to the right and left borders of a cell (only available if the **W**rap Text check box is selected).
Center across selection	Centers data across a range of cells.
Vertical	
Top	Aligns data at the cell's top border.
C**e**nter	Aligns data vertically at the cell's center.
Bottom	Aligns data at the bottom border of the cell.
Orie**n**tation	Selects an orientation style.
Wrap Text	Wraps text to another line in a cell if the data is too long.

Keyboard Steps

1. Select the cells you want to align.

2. Select the Forma**t** menu .... **Alt** + **T**

3. Select **A**lignment .... **A**

4. Select any alignment option from the preceding table by pressing .... **Alt** + *selection letter*

5. When finished selecting an alignment option, press .... ⏎

Mouse Steps

1. Select the cells to align.
2. Click on the Format menu.
3. Click on **Alignment**.
4. Click on any alignment option from the preceding table.
5. When finished selecting an alignment option, click on **OK**.

Data—Changing Font, Style, Size, Color and Effects

Changes the font, style, size, effects and color on selected data in a cell, range, or an entire document.

Keyboard Steps

1. Select the cells, range, or document in which you want to change fonts.
2. Select the Format menu .... `Alt` + `T`
3. Select Font .... `F`
4. Select any of the following options to change:
   Font .... `Alt` + `F`
   Font Style .... `Alt` + `Y`
   Color .... `Alt` + `C`
   Size .... `Alt` + `S`

5. **(Optional)** In the **Effects** box, select any of the following:
   Strikeout .... Alt + K
   Underline .... Alt + U

To reset the font, select Normal Font by pressing Alt+O.

6. To save the settings, press .... ⏎

Mouse Steps

1. Select the cells or document to change fonts.
2. Click on the Format menu.
3. Click on Font.

*In place of steps 2 and 3, you can click the right mouse button to bring up the shortcut menu, and select **Font**.*

4. Click on any of the following options to change:
   Font
   Font Style
   Color
   Size

5. **(Optional)** In the Effects box, click on any of the following:

   Strikeout

   Underline

To reset the font, click on the Normal Font check box.

6. To save the settings, click on **OK**.

*To change the font size quickly, click on the **Increase** and **Decrease Font Size** tools on the **Standard** toolbar.*

Data—Clearing

Removes the contents of a selected cell or range of cells (including values, text, data, formulas, notes, and formats).

There's a difference between the Edit Clear and Edit Delete commands. Edit Clear simply clears the contents (data) in a cell. Edit Delete deletes the contents and the cell itself, shifting the surrounding cells to eliminate the deleted cell.

Keyboard Steps

1. Select the cell(s) to clear.

2. Select the Edit menu .... `Alt` + `E`
3. Select Clear .... `E`

*You can also press the **Del** key to bring up the Clear dialog box.*

4. Select any of the following Clear options:
   All .... `Alt` + `A`
   Formats .... `Alt` + `T`
   Formulas .... `Alt` + `R`
   Notes .... `Alt` + `N`

5. When finished selecting a Clear option, press .... `↵`

Mouse Steps

1. Select the cell(s) to clear.
2. Click on the Edit menu.
3. Click on Clear.

*In place of steps 2 and 3, you can click the right mouse button to bring up the shortcut menu, and select **Clear**.*

4. Click on any of the following Clear options:
   All
   Formats
   Formulas
   Notes

5. When finished selecting a Clear option, click on **OK**.

Data—Copying

Copies data in selected cell(s) to the Windows Clipboard. The copied selections can be a single cell, range of cells, data, text, formulas, a chart, graphic object, or the entire document. Once the data is copied to the Clipboard, use the Paste command to copy the data back into the current Excel worksheet, another worksheet, or another application's document in the desired location.

Depending on the application you are pasting your data into, the information can look slightly different. For example, in Microsoft Word, the data will be pasted into a table.

When you copy cells containing formulas, be careful about how cells are referenced in the formulas. If a formula contains absolute references, any copy of that formula will be identical to the original, no matter where you copy it to. If a formula contains relative references, the references in a copy of the formula will change, depending on where you place the copy. For example, if you have a formula that has a relative reference to cell A1, and you copy the formula to a cell one row down and one column to the right of the original location, the relative reference will change to cell B2. For more information, see **Formula—Creating**, **Formula— Using Absolute References**, *and* **Formula—Using Relative References**.

Keyboard Steps

1. Select the cell(s) to copy into the Clipboard.
2. Select the Edit menu .... Alt + E
3. Select Copy C

*You can also press **Ctrl+C** or **Ctrl+Ins** to copy the selection to the Clipboard.*

TIP

4. Select a new location to which the selected cell(s) will be copied .... ↑ ↓ ← →
5. Select the Edit menu .... Alt + E
6. Select Paste .... P

54 Data—Copying

*You can paste the contents of the Clipboard quickly by pressing **Enter** in place of steps 5–7.*

7. To stop the flashing marquee, press .... Esc

Mouse Steps

1. Select the cell(s) to copy.
2. Click on the **Edit** menu.
3. Click on **Copy**.

*In place of steps 2 and 3, you can click the right mouse button to bring up the shortcut menu, and select **Copy**.*

4. Click on a new location to which the selected cell(s) will be copied.
5. Click on the **Edit** menu.
6. Click on **Paste**.

*To copy cells, click on the **Copy** tool from the **Standard** toolbar.*

Data—Copying 55

TIP *You can also copy by dragging. Select the cells you want to copy. Point to the selection border; press and hold the **Ctrl** key until a small plus (+) pointer appears. Drag to a new location, and then release the mouse button and **Ctrl** key.*

Data—Cutting and Moving

Removes the selected cell or range of cells from the document, and places them in the Windows Clipboard. You can then use the paste command to copy the data into Excel or another application.

*When you cut cells containing formulas and want to paste the cells to another worksheet location, cell references should remain absolute. For more information, see **Formula—Creating**, **Formula—Using Absolute References**, and **Formula—Using Relative References**.*

EXAMPLE *You can use the Cutting feature to move selected cells from one location to another in a document, or from one document to another.*

Keyboard Steps

1. Select the cell(s) to cut.
2. Select the Edit menu .... Alt + E
3. Select Cut .... T

Data—Copying

*You can also press **Shift+Del** or **Ctrl+X** to cut a selection to the Clipboard.*

4. Choose destination cell (or range) as the new location for the selected cell(s) .... ↑ ↓ ← →
5. Select the Edit menu .... Alt + E
6. Select Paste .... P

*You can paste the contents of the Clipboard quickly by pressing **Enter** in place of steps 5–7.*

Mouse Steps

1. Select the cell(s) to cut.
2. Click on the Edit menu.
3. Click on Cut.

In place of steps 2 and 3, you can click the right mouse button to bring up the shortcut menu, and select Cut.

4. Click on a destination cell to be the new location for the selected cell(s).

Data—Cutting and Moving

5. Click on the **Edit** menu.
6. Click on **Paste**.

*You can click on the **Cut** tool (on the **Custom** toolbar) to cut the selected cell(s).*

You can also move by dragging. Select the cells you want to move. Point to the selection border so the mouse pointer turns into an arrow. Press and hold the left mouse button, drag the selection to a new location, and release the mouse button.

Data—Finding and Replacing

Searches an entire document or a selected range for specified text or values, and replaces the found data with other text or values you specify.

If you only want to find text and not necessarily replace it, you can use the Formula Find command.

Keyboard Steps

1. Select the range of cells to search.

EXAMPLE *If you want to search the entire worksheet, do not select a range.*

2. Select the Formula menu .... `Alt` + `R`

3. Select Replace .... `E`

4. In the Find What box,
   enter the data to search for .... `Alt` + `N`
   text or *number*

5. In the Replace With dialog
   box, enter the replacement
   data .... `Alt` + `W`
   replacement text

6. In the Look at box, select
   to find all or part of the
   search characters:
   Whole .... `Alt` + `E`
   Part .... `Alt` + `P`

7. Select to search by:
   Rows .... `Alt` + `O`
   Columns .... `Alt` + `L`

8. **(Optional)** For a case-sensitive
   search, select Match Case .... `Alt` + `C`

9. Select any of the following
   options:
   To Replace All of the matches,
   press .... `Alt` + `A`

Data—Finding and Replacing

To keep the contents of the
cell and find the next occur-
rence, select Find Next .... Alt + F
To replace the contents of
the cell and find the next
occurrence, select Replace .... Alt + R

10. When finished replacing,
    select Close .... Esc

Mouse Steps

1. Select the range of cells to search.

If you want to search the entire worksheet, do not select a range.

2. Click on the Formula menu.

3. Click on Replace.

4. Click in the Find What box, and enter the data to search.

5. Click in the Replace With dialog box, and enter the data to replace with.

6. In the Look at box, select whether to find the Whole or Part of the set of search characters.

7. Select (click on) whether to search by Rows or Columns.

8. **(Optional)** For a case-sensitive search, click on Match **C**ase.

9. Select any of the following options:
   To replace all of the matches, click on Replace **A**ll.
   To keep the contents of the cell and find the next occurrence, click on **F**ind Next.
   To replace the contents of the cell and find the next occurrence, click on **R**eplace.

10. When finished replacing, click on Close.

Data—Insert Paste

Inserts the Clipboard's contents (cells, ranges, rows, or columns) between existing cells. The cells will shift to accommodate the insertion.

Keyboard Steps

1. Using the Edit **C**opy or the Edit Cu**t** commands, insert data into the Clipboard.

2. Select the cell to insert (paste) the Clipboard's contents into .... ⬆ ⬇ ⬅ ➡

3. Select the **E**dit menu .... Alt + E

4. Select **I**nsert Paste I

Data—Insert Paste

5. Select one of the following options:
   Shift Cell **R**ight .... Alt + R
   Shift Cells **D**own .... Alt + D

Mouse Steps

1. Using the Edit Copy or the Edit Cut commands, insert data into the Clipboard.

2. Select the cell to paste the Clipboard's contents into.

3. Click on the Edit menu.

4. Click on Insert Paste.

5. Click on one of the following options:
   Shift Cell **R**ight
   Shift Cells **D**own

Data—Pasting

Copies (pastes) the contents of the Windows Clipboard into a specified cell.

When you paste cells containing formulas, be careful about how cells are referenced in the formulas. If a formula contains absolute references, any copy of that formula will be identical to the original, no matter where you copy it to. If a formula contains relative references, the references in a copy of the formula will change, depending on where you place the copy. For example, if you have a formula that has a relative reference to cell A1, and you copy the formula to a cell one row down and one column to the right of the original location, the relative reference will change to cell B2. Pasting formulas that were cut doesn't affect cell references. For more information, see **Formula—Creating**, **Formula—Using Absolute References**, *and* **Formula—Using Relative References**.

Keyboard Steps

1. Using the **Edit Copy** or the **Edit Cut** commands, insert data into the Clipboard.

2. Select the cell to paste the Clipboard's contents to .... [↑] [↓] [←] [→]

You can also open another Excel document (or go to another application), and paste the contents of the Clipboard.

3. Select the Edit menu .... [Alt] + [E]
4. Select Paste .... [P]

You can also press **Enter**, **Ctrl+V**, *or* **Shift+Ins** *to paste the Clipboard's contents into the worksheet.*

Data—Pasting

Mouse Steps

1. Insert data into the Clipboard using the **Edit Copy** or the **Edit Cut** commands.
2. Select the cell to paste the Clipboard's contents to.
3. Click on the **Edit** menu.
4. Click on **Paste**.

*In place of steps 2 and 3, you can click the right mouse button to bring up the shortcut menu, and select **Paste**.*

*You can click on the **Paste** tool (found on the **Custom** toolbar) to paste the Clipboard's contents into the worksheet.*

Data—Protecting

Adds protection or security to the data in a selected cell (or range of cells), to prevent editing of the data or formulas.

Keyboard Steps

1. Select the cell(s) to protect.

TIP *To select the entire worksheet to protect, press **Ctrl+Shift+Spacebar**.*

2. Select the Format menu .... `Alt` + `T`
3. Select Cell Protection .... `I`
4. **(Optional)** Select the Locked option to prevent editing .... `Alt` + `L`
5. Select the Hidden option to hide formulas .... `Alt` + `I`
6. When finished, press .... `↵`
7. Select the Options menu to turn on protection .... `Alt` + `O`
8. Select Protect Document .... `P`
9. **(Optional)** Select the Cells check box .... `Alt` + `C`
10. Press .... `↵`

Mouse Steps

1. Select the cell(s) to protect.
2. Click on the Format menu.
3. Click on Cell Protection.

4. **(Optional)** Click on the Locked option to prevent editing.

5. Click on the Hidden option to hide formulas.

6. When finished, click on **OK**.

7. To turn on protection, click on the Options menu.

8. Click on **P**rotect Document.

9. **(Optional)** Click on the Cells check box.

10. Click on **OK**.

Data—Styles

Applies a cell style to the data in the selected cells or worksheet.

A **style** *is simply a named combination of cell formats.*

Keyboard Steps

1. Select the range of cells to apply the style.

2. Select the Format menu .... Alt + T

3. Select Style .... S

4. Select a style from the Style
   Name drop-down list .... Alt + S
   ↑ or ↓

5. When finished, press .... ⏎

EXAMPLE

To define or edit a style in the list, select the Define button by pressing D.

Mouse Steps

1. Select the range of cells to apply the style.
2. Click on the Format menu.
3. Click on Style.
4. Click on a style from the Style Name drop-down list.
5. When finished, click on **OK**.

TIP

To define or edit a style in the list, click on the Define button.

TIP

*You can apply a style quickly by clicking on the **Style** drop-down list box on the **Standard** toolbar (or the **Formatting** toolbar), and clicking on a style.*

Data—Styles 67

Data Form

Allows you to view the database records one record at a time, so you can edit, delete, and add records to the database. The following table lists the options available in the Data Form.

Data Form Dialog Box Buttons

Button	Description
Close	Closes the Data Form dialog box.
Criteria	Displays a dialog box where you can search for specific records.
Delete	Deletes the selected record.
Find Next	Finds the next matching record after criteria are specified.
Find Prev	Finds the previous matching record after criteria are specified.
Form	Returns to the Data Form from the Criteria Form.
New	Adds a new record.
Restore	Restores data to its state prior to editing.
Clear	Clears the current entry from the Criteria form.

Keyboard Steps

1. Define the database range using the **D**ata **S**et **D**atabase command (see **Database—Defining** for instructions).

2. Select the **D**ata menu .... `Alt` + `D`

3. Select F**o**rm .... `O`

4. When viewing, adding, editing, or deleting a database record, select one of the buttons in the preceding table by pressing .... `Alt` + *selection letter*

5. When finished with Data Form, select C**l**ose .... `Alt` + `L` or `Esc`

Mouse Steps

1. Define the database range using the **D**ata Set Database command (see **Database—Defining** for instructions).

2. Click on the **D**ata menu.

3. Click on F**o**rm.

4. When viewing, adding, editing, or deleting a database record, click on a button listed in the preceding table.

5. When finished with Data Form, click on Close.

Database—Defining

Creates a database from a selected range of cells.

*Before you define your database, you need to enter the data for it into your worksheet. The first row of the data must hold the **field names** (which identify the different data types you're recording for each entry). For example, Fname and Lname are common field names for entering first and last names. For each entry, you'll need to fill in the fields across one row. For example, you would type one person's first name and last name in the Fname and Lname columns of one row. Each row or entry is called a **record**. The remaining rows can contain data or be blank. The last row should be blank to allow the database to grow. Note that you can also add data to the database using the Data Form (after you've defined the database).*

Keyboard Steps

1. Select the range of cells in the worksheet that will make up the database, including a blank row at the end.
2. Select the **D**ata menu .... Alt + D
3. Select Set Data**b**ase .... B

Mouse Steps

1. Select the range of cells in the worksheet that will make up the database, including a blank row at the end.
2. Click on the **D**ata menu.

Database—Defining

3. Click on Set Database.

Database—Defining an Extract Range

*You can extract data from a database to another part of the worksheet, on the conditions you specify in the criteria range (see **Database—Setting Criteria**). The data is copied into the extract range, and is not deleted from the database.*

If your database lists your clients and the last date they were contacted, and you want to see a list of only those clients contacted more than three months ago, you can use an extract range to list them.

Keyboard Steps

1. Copy the database field names into the area on the worksheet you would like to extract the information to, leaving extra blank cells beneath the field names.

2. Select the target range that you want to extract the records into, including the field names you just copied in step 1.

3. Select the Data menu .... Alt + D
4. Select the Set Extract X

Mouse Steps

1. Copy the database field names into the area on the worksheet you would like to extract the information to, leaving extra blank cells beneath the field names.

2. Select the target range that you want to extract the records into, including the field names you just copied in step 1.

3. Click on the Data menu.

4. Click on the Set Extract.

Database—Deleting Records

Deletes database records that match the criteria in the criteria range. These steps let you delete multiple records in a single operation.

*Be careful when deleting a record, because you **cannot** reverse the deletion process.*

Database—Defining an Extract Range

Keyboard Steps

1. Define the criteria and criteria range using the Data Set Criteria command. (See **Database—Defining an Extract Range** and **Database—Setting Criteria**.)

*Do **not** include blank rows in the criteria range; it results in the deletion of **all** records in the database.*

2. Select the Data menu .... Alt + D
3. Select Delete .... D
4. To delete the records, press .... ↵

Mouse Steps

1. Using the Data Set Criteria command, define the criteria and the criteria range. (See **Database—Defining an Extract Range** and **Database—Setting Criteria**.)

*Do **not** include blank rows in the criteria range; it results in the deletion of **all** records in the database.*

Database—Deleting Records

2. Click on the **Data** menu.

3. Click on **Delete**.

4. To delete the records, click on **OK**.

Database—Extracting Data

Extracts (copies) specified data from a database and places it in a defined range.

EXAMPLE

If you have a client database and you need a list of clients in the Chicago area, you can extract their names into an extract range without searching for them individually. You would set a criterion to tell Excel you want only those clients with the word "Chicago" in the "City" field. You would then set the Extract range to tell Excel where you want the new database created. Finally, you would use the Data Extract command to extract the data.

Keyboard Steps

1. Define the database (see **Database—Defining**).

2. Set the Criteria range (see **Database—Setting Criteria**).

3. Set the Extract range (see **Database—Setting Extract Range**).

4. Select the Data menu .... `Alt` + `D`

5. Select Extract .... `E`

Mouse Steps

1. Define the database (see **Database—Defining**).

2. Set the Criteria range (see **Database—Setting Criteria**).

3. Set the Extract range (see **Database—Setting Extract Range**).

4. Click on the Data menu.

5. Click on Extract.

Database—Finding Data

*Finds records in the database that meet the criteria you specify in the criteria range. (To set the criteria range, see **Database—Setting Criteria**.)*

Keyboard Steps

1. Using the Data Set Criteria command, define the criteria and the criteria range.

2. Enter your criteria in the range .... ***criteria***

3. Select the Data menu .... `Alt` + `D`

4. Select **Find** .... F

5. To find the next or preceding record that meets the criteria, press .... ↑ or ↓

Excel will enter the Find mode when using the Find command. To exit the Find mode, select the Data Exit Find command.

Mouse Steps

1. Define the criteria and the criteria range using the **Data Set Criteria** command.
2. Enter your criteria in the range.
3. Click on the **Data** menu.
4. Click on **Find**.
5. To find the next or preceding record that meets the criteria, click on the up and down scroll arrows.

Database—Setting Criteria

Before you can search a database for specific records, you must first tell Excel what to search for by setting the criteria.

EXAMPLE *If you have a client database and you need a list of clients in the Chicago area, you can extract their names into an extract range without searching for them individually. You would tell Excel you want only those clients with the word "Chicago" in the "City" field by entering* **Chicago** *below the* **City** *field in the criteria range.*

Criteria Operators

Operator	Description
=	Equal to
>	Greater than

Operator	Description
<	Less than
>=	Greater than or equal to
<=	Less than or equal to
<>	Not equal to

Keyboard Steps

1. Copy the field names into a range of cells that have extra blank cells beneath them.

2. Under the appropriate field name, enter the criteria you want to search for in the database. You can use any of the operators listed in the table above.

Database—Setting Criteria

For example, you could enter >50 to find all records that contain a value that is greater than 50 in the specified field.

3. Select the range of cells that will make up the criteria range, including the names created in step 1, and the criteria from step 2.

4. Select the **Data** menu .... Alt + D
5. Select Set **Criteria** C

Mouse Steps

1. Copy the field names into a range of cells that have extra blank cells beneath them.

2. Under the appropriate field name, enter the criteria you want to search for in the database. You can use any operators listed in the preceding table.

For example, you could enter >50 to find all records that contain a value greater than 50 in the specified field.

3. Select the range of cells that will make up the criteria range, including the names created in step 1, and the criteria from step 2.

4. Click on the **Data** menu.

5. Click on Set **Criteria**.

Database—Sorting Records

*Organizes or rearranges the database records in ascending or descending order, alphabetically or numerically. You can sort on multiple fields; each field to sort is called a **key**. You can have a single-, two-, or three-key sort.*

*If you wanted a list of your clients alphabetized by city, and then by Last name and first name, you would use a **three-key sort**. The **1st key** is the key that all records are sorted on, the **City** field. All records that have the same city are sorted by the **2nd key**, the **Last name** field. Finally, if there are records that have the same city and the same last name, these records are sorted by the **3rd key**, the **First name** field.*

Keyboard Steps

1. Select the rows or columns of records in the database to sort. **DO NOT** select the field names.

2. Select the **D**ata menu ....`Alt` + `D`

3. Select **S**ort ....`S`

4. In the Sort By box, select
   to sort by **R**ows or
   Columns ....`Alt` + `R` or `Alt` + `C`

5. If you selected **R**ows:
   in the **1**st Key box, enter the
   address for a cell that's in the
   column you want to sort by ....`Alt` + `1`
   cell address

   OR

   If you selected **C**olumns:
   in the **1**st Key box, enter the
   address for a cell that's in the
   row you want to sort by ....`Alt` + `1`
   cell address

   > **TIP**
   > *Using the arrow keys, you can simply highlight a cell in the row or column you want to sort by. The cell reference in the appropriate Key box changes automatically.*

6. Select to sort in
   Ascending or
   Descending order ....`Alt` + `A` or `Alt` + `D`

   OR

   Press ....`↑` or `↓`

Database—Sorting Records

7. When finished selecting
   sort options, press .... ⏎

Mouse Steps

1. Select the rows or columns of records in the database to sort. **DO NOT** select the field names.

2. Click on the **D**ata menu.

3. Click on **S**ort.

4. In the Sort By box, click on **R**ows or **C**olumns to sort by.

You can simply click with the mouse to highlight a cell in the row or column you want to sort by. The cell reference in the appropriate Key box changes automatically.

5. If you selected **R**ows, click in the **1**st Key box and enter a column to sort.

   OR

   If you selected **C**olumns, click in the **1**st Key box and enter a row to sort.

   Sort by number

Database—Sorting Records

6. Click on **Ascending** or **Descending** order.

7. When finished selecting sort options, click on **OK**.

 *To sort the database records quickly, you can also click on the **Ascending** and **Descending** sort tools in the **Utility** toolbar.*

Display Options—Setting

Allows you to control the way the columns and rows are displayed in the worksheet, by turning options (such as gridlines, row and column headings, and formulas) on and off. The following table is a list of the display options available.

Display Options	Description
Formulas	Displays formulas or result of formulas cells.
Gridlines	Displays lines around a cell.
Row & Column Headings	Displays column letters and row numbers.
Zero Values	Displays either a 0 for zero values or blank.

Display Options	Description
Outline Symbols	Displays symbols used in outlines.
Automatic Page Breaks	Displays page breaks.
Show All	Displays objects created using Toolbar options.
Show Placeholders	Displays pictures and charts as gray rectangles.
Hide All	Hides all objects created using Toolbar options.
Gridline and Heading Color	Displays selected colors for gridlines and headings.

Keyboard Steps

1. Select the Options menu .... **Alt** + **O**
2. Select Display .... **D**
3. Select display options from the preceding table .... **Alt** + *selection letter*
4. When finished selecting options, press .... ⏎

Display Options—Setting

Mouse Steps

1. Click on the **O**ptions menu.
2. Click on **D**isplay.
3. Click on display options from the preceding table.
4. When finished selecting options, click on **OK**.

Exiting

Closes all open documents, exits Excel, and returns you to the Windows Program Manager.

If you have not saved any of the open documents before exiting, Excel will ask you if you want to save the document. Select Yes to save, or No not to save.

Keyboard Steps

1. Select the **F**ile menu .... **Alt** + **F**
2. Select E**x**it .... **X**

A shortcut to exiting Excel is to press Alt+F4.

Mouse Steps

1. Click on the File menu.
2. Click on Exit.

*A shortcut to exiting Excel is to double-click on the **Control menu** box.*

File—Closing

The Close command closes the document in the active window without exiting Excel.

If you have not saved your changes to the active file, Excel will ask you if you want to save the file. Answer Yes to save, or No not to save.

Keyboard Steps

1. Select the File menu .... Alt + F
2. Select Close C

Mouse Steps

1. Click on the File menu.
2. Click on Close.

*As a shortcut, you can close the file by double-clicking on the window's **Control menu**.*

File—Closing All

*Closes all open windows in Excel. This command will appear only on the File menu, when you press and hold the **Shift** key before pulling down the menu.*

Keyboard Steps

1. Select the File menu .... `Alt` + `Shift` + `F`
2. Select Close All .... `C`

Mouse Steps

1. Press the Shift key and click on the File menu.
2. Click on Close All.

File—Deleting

Deletes a file from your disk. Be very sure before deleting a file. Once you have deleted a file, you can't retrieve it.

Keyboard Steps

1. Select the File menu .... `Alt` + `F`
2. Select Delete .... `D`

TIP *If you need to change to another directory, press **Alt+D** to select the Directories list box, and select a directory. To select a different drive, press **Alt+V** to select the Drives list box, and select a drive.*

3. Select the file to delete from the Files Name list box .... `Alt` + `N`
   `↑` or `↓`

4. To delete the selected file, press .... `↵`

5. Excel will ask if you are sure you want to delete the file. Press .... `↵`

Mouse Steps

1. Click on the **File** menu.
2. Click on **Delete**.

TIP *If you need to change to another directory, click on the Directories list box and select a directory. To select a different drive, click on the Drives list box and select a drive.*

3. In the Files Name list box, click on a file to delete.
4. To delete the selected file, click on **OK**.

File—Deleting

5. Excel will ask if you are sure you want to delete the file. Click on **Yes**.

File—New

Creates a new worksheet, chart, macro sheet, workbook document, or slide show.

Keyboard Steps

1. Select the File menu .... `Alt` + `F`
2. Select New .... `N`
3. Select one of the following
   types of files to create: .... `↑` or `↓`
   Worksheet
   Chart
   Macro Sheet
   Workbook
   Slides
4. To create a new file, press .... `↵`

*To create a new worksheet quickly, press **Alt+Shift+F1** or **Shift+F11**.*

Mouse Steps

1. Click on the File menu.
2. Click on New.

3. Click on one of the following types of files to create:

   Worksheet
   Chart
   Macro Sheet
   Workbook
   Slides

4. To create a new file, click on **OK**.

*To create a new worksheet quickly, click on the **New Worksheet** tool on the **Standard** toolbar.*

File—Opening

Opens a previously saved Excel file.

Keyboard Steps

1. Select the File menu .... Alt + F
2. Select Open .... O

*If you need to change to another directory, press **Alt+D** to select the Directories list box, and select a directory. To select a different drive, press **Alt+V** to select the Drives list box, and select a drive.*

3. From the Files Name list
   box, select a file to open .... Alt + N
   ↑ or ↓

4. To open the selected file, press .... ↵

*To open a previously saved file quickly, press **Ctrl+F12** or **Alt+Ctrl+F2**.*

Mouse Steps

1. Click on the File menu.

2. Click on Open.

*If you need to change to another directory, click on the **Directories** list box and select a directory. To select a different drive, click on the **Drives** list box and select a drive.*

3. Click on a file to open in the Files Name list box.

4. To open the selected file, click on **OK**.

*To open a previously saved file quickly, click on the **Open** tool on the **Standard** toolbar.*

File—Save

Saves the active document to a named file in the directory of the disk you specify.

Keyboard Steps

1. Display the document to save in the active window.

2. Select the File menu .... **Alt** + **F**

3. Select Save .... **S**

4. If you have not saved the file previously, the Save As dialog box appears, asking you to name the file (see **File—Save As**).
   Type a file name .... ***filename***
   Press .... **↵**

TIP

*To save a file quickly, press **Shift+F12** or **Alt+Shift+F2**.*

Mouse Steps

1. Display the document to save in the active window.

2. Click on the File menu.

3. Click on Save.

4. If you have not saved the file previously, the Save As dialog box appears, asking you to name the file (see **File—Save As**). Type a file name and click on **OK**.

To save a file quickly, click on the Save tool from the Standard toolbar.

File—Saving with a New Name

Allows you to name a new file, or rename a previously saved file and save it to the disk.

If you updated the file called BUDGET92.XLS with 1993 data, use the Save As command to save the file with a new name called BUDGET93.XLS, without overwriting the 1992 file.

Keyboard Steps

1. In the active window, display the document to save.
2. Select the File menu .... `Alt` + `F`
3. Select Save As .... `A`

*If you need to change to another directory, press **Alt+D** to select the **Directories** list box, and select a directory. To select a different drive, press **Alt+V** to select the Drives list box, and select a drive. To select a different file format, press **Alt+T** to select the Save File as Type drop-down list, and select a file type.*

4. Enter a file name .... ***filename***

5. **(Optional)** To set a password or create backup files, select the Options button .... Alt + O

6. When ready to save the file, press .... ⏎

*To save a file quickly in the **File Save As** dialog box, press **F12**.*

Mouse Steps

1. Display the document to save in the active window.

2. Click on the File menu.

3. Click on Save As.

If you need to save the file to another directory, click on the Directories list box and select a directory. To select a different drive, click on

File—Saving with a New Name 93

the Drives list box and select a drive. To select a different file format, click on the Save File as Type drop-down list.

4. Enter a file name.

5. **(Optional)** To set a password or create backup files, click on the **O**ptions button.

6. When ready to save the file, click on **OK**.

Formula—Creating

*Formulas perform mathematical calculations on numbers and return results. Note that all formulas **must** begin with an = (equals sign). You can also use **functions** (predefined Excel formulas) in formulas. See Appendix A for a list of the common Excel functions.*

Operator	Description
+	Addition
-	Subtraction
*	Multiplication
/	Division
%	Percent
^	Exponent
&	Combines more than one text value
:	Ranges

For example, you want to know what your home's average monthly utility bills were last year.

Cell B1 contains the total electric bills ($500) and cell B2 contains the total gas bills ($350). You want the average to be placed in cell B3. The formula in cell B3 to calculate this average would look like =(B1+B2)/12 with the result of $70.83. Notice the ( ) (parenthesis). If you did not include the parenthesis, B3 would first be divided by 12 and then added to B2 which would result in the total of $529.17.

EXAMPLE *You can use functions to speed up the entering of formulas. For example, you want to add all of your expenses for the month of January which are listed in cells A1 through A10 to be totaled in cell A11. The formula in cell A11 would look like =SUM(A1:A11).*

Keyboard Steps

1. Select the cell where you want the result of the formula to appear.

2. Press the = (equals sign) .... =

3. **(Optional)** Enter the opening parenthesis if necessary .... (

4. Type a cell address, or select the cell for the first number in the formula .... ***cell address***
   ↑ or ↓

Formula—Creating 95

5. Enter a mathematical operand (see table on page 94).

6. Select the cell for the next number .... ⬆ or ⬇

   OR

   Enter a number .... ***number***

7. **(Optional)** Enter the closing parenthesis if necessary ....)

8. Repeat steps 3–5 if necessary to complete the formula.

9. When finished with the formula, press .... ↵

Mouse Steps

1. Select the cell where you want the result of the formula to appear.

2. Enter the equals sign (=).

3. Type a cell address or click on the cell for the first number in the formula.

4. Enter a mathematical operand (see table on page 94).

5. Select the cell or enter a number for the next number.

6. Repeat steps 3–5 if necessary to complete the formula.

7. When finished with the formula, click on the **Enter** tool.

TIP

To enter a cell range, type a colon (:) between the first and last cells in the range. For example, to calculate the sum of values in cells B1 through B12, enter the formula =SUM(B1:B12).

Formula—Using Absolute References

You can enter mathematical expressions which calculate to create new results. When you create a formula that uses absolute references to cells, the cell references do not change if you move or copy the cell.

EXAMPLE

*If you are trying to copy the cell that holds the formula for the sum of all your column A numbers [=SUM(A1:A9)] to a cell in column B, Excel adjusts the formula so it adds all the numbers in column B [=SUM(B1:B9)]. If you want Excel to keep exactly the same formula, no matter where you copy it, you have to make the references **absolute** by inserting dollar signs before the column letters and row numbers [=SUM($A$1:$A$9)].*

Keyboard Steps

1. Select the cell in which to enter a formula.

2. Press the = (equals sign) .... =

3. Enter the desired formula. In each cell address you want to designate as absolute, enter a $ (dollar sign) before its column letter and/or row number .... *formula*

After entering a cell reference, press F4 and Excel will convert it to an absolute reference for you.

TIP

4. Press ....

Mouse Steps

1. Select the cell in which to enter a formula.

2. Press the = (equals sign) key.

3. Enter the desired formula. In each cell address you want to designate as absolute, enter a $ (dollar sign) before its column letter and/or row number.

4. Click on the Enter tool, which looks like a check mark to the left of the formular bar.

Formula—Using Relative References

You can enter mathematical expressions which calculate to create new results. When you create a formula that uses relative references to cells, the cell references change if you move or copy the cell.

EXAMPLE *You've created the formula =(A1+A2) in cell A3. Now you want to add the numbers in cells B1 and B2. When you copy cell A3 to B3, Excel will adjust the formula to add **B1** and **B2** instead of A1 and A2. In cell B3, you'll see the formula =**(B1+B2)**. Excel used the formula in cell A3, it just changed the cell references to add the numbers in the B column.*

Keyboard Steps

1. Select the cell in which to enter a formula.

2. Press the = (equals sign) key .... =

3. Enter the desired formula ....*formula*

4. Press .... ↵

Mouse Steps

1. Select the cell in which to enter a formula.

2. Press the = (equals sign) key.

3. Enter the desired formula.

4. Click on the Enter tool, which looks like a check mark to the left of the formula bar.

Formula—Goal Seeking

Changes the values in a cell with a formula to meet a specific goal.

For example, if you want to purchase a house in the next 5 years, and you have a savings goal of $15,000 for the down payment, you can have Excel tell you how much money you need to save per month to meet that goal. You could enter a formula in cell C4 that reads **=A4*12*5**. This would take the value in A4 and multiply it by 12 payments per month for 5 years. Then you can select cell C4, choose Formula Goal Seek, set the **To Value** box to **15000** and the **By changing cell** box to A4, and then choose OK.

Keyboard Steps

1. Select the cell which contains the formulas.

2. Select the Formula menu .... [Alt] + [R]

3. Select Goal Seek .... [L]

4. In the To value box,
   enter the goal .... [Alt] + [V]
   ####

5. In the By changing cell box, enter the cell address of the value to change .... `Alt` + `C` *cell address*

6. To begin the goal-seek procedure, press .... `↵`

7. To accept the change, press .... `↵`

   OR

   To reject the change, press Cancel .... `Esc`

Mouse Steps

1. Select the cell that contains the formulas.

2. Click on the Formula menu.

3. Click on Goal Seek.

4. Click in the To value box, and enter the goal.

5. Click in the By changing cell box, and enter the cell address of the value to change (by clicking on the cell to change in the worksheet).

6. To begin the goal-seek procedure, click on **OK**.

7. To accept the change, click on **OK**.

   OR

   To reject the change, click on Cancel.

Formula—Goal Seeking

Formula—Pasting Functions

Pastes a predefined Excel function into the formula being created in the formula bar. Using the Paste Function command is the easiest way to use a function, because you don't have to remember the function's name and arguments.

Keyboard Steps

1. Select the cell to hold the formula. Begin typing the formula if necessary.
2. Select the Formula menu .... **Alt** + **R**
3. Select Paste Function .... **T**

*To select Paste Function quickly, press **Shift+F3**.*

TIP

4. In the Function Category box, select a category .... **Alt** + **C**
   ↑ or ↓
5. In the Paste Function box, select a function .... **Alt** + **F**
   ↑ or ↓
6. **(Optional)** To include the arguments, select Paste Arguments .... **Alt** + **A**

7. To paste the function in
   the formula bar, press ....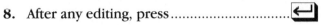

8. After any editing, press .... ⏎

Mouse Steps

1. Select the cell to hold the formula. Begin typing the formula if necessary.

2. Click on the Formula menu.

3. Click on Paste Function.

4. In the Function Category box, click on a category.

5. In the Paste Function box, click on a function.

6. **(Optional)** To include the arguments, click on Paste Arguments.

7. To paste the function in the formula bar, click on **OK**.

8. After any editing, click on **OK**.

*To select Paste Function quickly, click on the **Paste Function** tool from the **Custom** toolbar.*

TIP

Formula—Pasting Functions

Formula—Pasting Names

*Pastes a defined range name into the formula being created in the formula bar. (To define a range name, see **Range—Defining Names**.)*

Keyboard Steps

1. Select the cell to hold the formula. Begin typing the formula if necessary .... ***formula***

2. Select the Formula menu .... `Alt` + `R`

3. Select **P**aste Name .... `P`

4. In the Paste Name box, select a name to paste .... `Alt` + `N`
   `↑` or `↓`

5. To paste a name, press .... `↵`

Mouse Steps

1. Select the cell to hold the formula. Begin typing the formula if necessary.

2. Click on the Formula menu.

3. Click on **P**aste Name.

4. In the Paste Name box, click on a name to paste.

5. To paste a name, click on **OK**.

Formula—Protecting

See **Data—Protecting**.

Formula—Setting Calculation Options

Specifies how calculations on formulas will be performed in a worksheet or chart.

Keyboard Steps

1. Select the Options menu .... `Alt` + `O`
2. Select Calculation .... `C`
3. Select a calculation method from the **Calculation** box:

Option	Description
Automatic	Recalculates formulas automatically when a change occurs in a document.
Automatic Except Table	Recalculates formulas automatically except for tables (which take longer to calculate).

continues

continued

Option	Description
Manual	Allows you to calculate formulas manually.
Recalculate Before Save	Recalculates formulas automatically every time a document is saved.

4. Select desired options from the **Sheet Option** box:
   Update **R**emote Reference .... `Alt` + `R`
   Precision as Displayed .... `Alt` + `P`
   1904 **D**ate System .... `Alt` + `D`
   Save External **L**ink Values .... `Alt` + `L`
   Alternate E**x**pression
   Evaluation .... `Alt` + `X`
   Alternate **F**ormula Entry .... `Alt` + `F`

5. **(Optional)** Select the Calc Now button to recalculate formulas in all open documents now .... `Alt` + `N`

6. **(Optional)** Select the Calc Document button to calculate the active document now .... `Alt` + `O`

7. When completed setting calculation options, press .... `↵`

106 Formula—Setting Calculation Options

Mouse Steps

1. Click on the **O**ptions menu.
2. Click on **C**alculation.
3. Click on a calculation method in the Calculation box.

Option	Description
Automatic	Recalculates formulas automatically when a change occurs in a document.
Automatic Except **T**able	Recalculates formulas automatically except for tables (which take longer to calculate).
Manual	Allows you to calculate formulas manually.
Recalculate Before Save	Recalculates formulas automatically every time a document is saved.

4. Click on the desired options from the Sheet Option box:
   Update **R**emote Reference
   Precision as Displayed

Formula—Setting Calculation Options

1904 Date System
Save External Link Values
Alternate Expression Evaluation
Alternate Formula Entry

5. **(Optional)** Click on the Calc **N**ow button to recalculate formulas in all open documents now.

6. **(Optional)** Click on the Calc D**o**cument button to calculate the active document now.

7. When finished setting calculation options, click on **OK**.

Formula—Solver

Solves a formula for a maximum, minimum, or specified result. Solver adjusts data to answer questions such as "What do I need to adjust to meet my budget?" or "How many more units do I have to sell to make my profit margin?"

Let's say you have $5,000 to spend on the inventory of your computer software store. You sell three software packages, at different prices. You will need to know how many of each to stock up on, without going over the $5,000 budget. The cells would contain the following data and formulas:

A1 100

A2 200

A3 300

B1 4

B2 5

B3 6
C1 =A1*B1
C2 =A2*B2
C3 =A3*B3
C4 =SUM(C1:C3)

*In the **Solver** dialog box, enter cell **C4** in the **Set Cell** text box and **5000** in the **Equal to Values of** text box. You would then tell Excel to change the values in cell **B1:B10** in the **By Changing Cells** text box. Excel will change the quantities until it reaches the $5,000 total amount, giving the total number of software packages you can have in stock for $5,000.*

Keyboard Steps

1. Select the cell to maximize, minimize, or reach a target result.

2. Select the Formula menu .... **Alt** + **R**

3. Select Solver .... **V**

4. Select one of the following options:
   Max .... **Alt** + **M**
   Min .... **Alt** + **N**
   Value .... **Alt** + **V**

5. If you selected Value, enter a desired target value .... #####

Formula—Solver

6. In the **B**y Changing Cells box, enter the cells to adjust until a solution is reached .... `Alt` + `B` `↑` or `↓`

7. **(Optional)** Specify any constraints to specific cells by selecting the **A**dd button .... `Alt` + `A`

8. To begin solving, select the **S**olve button .... `Alt` + `S`

To clear all of the settings, select the Reset All button by pressing Alt+R.

TIP

Mouse Steps

1. Select the cell to maximize, minimize, or reach a target result.

2. Click on the Formula menu.

3. Click on Solver.

4. Click on one of the following options:
   Max
   Min
   Value

5. If you selected the Value option, enter a desired target value.

6. In the **B**y Changing Cells box, enter the cells to adjust.

7. **(Optional)** Specify any constraints to specific cells by clicking on the Add button.

8. To begin solving, click on the Solve button.

To clear all of the settings, click on the Reset All button.

Graphic Object—Bringing to Front

Brings an object from the background to the foreground, in front of all other overlapping objects. This requires a mouse.

Mouse Steps

1. Click on the object in the background to bring to front.

2. Click on the Format menu.

3. Click on Bring to Front.

Instead of steps 2 and 3, you can click the right mouse button to display the shortcut menu, and click on Bring to Front.

Graphic Object—Copying

Makes a copy of a graphic object. This requires a mouse.

Mouse Steps

1. Click on the graphic object to copy.
2. Point anywhere on the graphic object.
3. Press and hold the Ctrl key and drag the pointer to a new location.
4. Release the mouse button.

Graphic Object—Creating

*Graphic objects in a worksheet are arrows, lines, rectangles, ovals, circles, and text boxes you draw on the worksheet, using the tools on the Drawing toolbar. (To create graphic objects, see: **Chart—Creating**, **Drawing—Objects**, **Chart—Adding Arrows**, or **Macro—Assigning to Object**.)*

Graphic Object—Deleting

Deletes a graphic object from a worksheet. This requires a mouse.

Mouse Steps

1. Click on the graphic object to delete.
2. Click on Delete.

Graphic Object—Formatting

Adds or changes formatting to a graphic object. This requires a mouse.

Mouse Steps

1. Click on the object to format.
2. Click on the Format menu.
3. Click on **P**attern.

*In place of steps 2 and 3, you can click the right mouse button to bring up the shortcut menu, and select **Pattern**.*

4. To change the border on the object, click on an option in the Border box:
   Automatic
   None
   Style
   Color
   Weight

5. Select a Fill option:
   Automatic
   Non**e**
   Pattern
   Foreground
   Background

6. To create a border shadow, click in the Sha**d**ow check box.

7. To save the settings, click on **OK**.

Graphic Object—Formatting

Graphic Object—Grouping

Groups several graphic objects together, to create a single graphic object. This requires a mouse.

Mouse Steps

1. As you select the objects you want to group (see **Graphic Object—Selecting**), press and hold the **Shift** key.
2. Click on the Format menu.
3. Click on Group.

To ungroup objects, select Ungroup by pressing U.

Graphic Object—Moving

Moves a graphic object to a new location. This requires a mouse.

Mouse Steps

1. Click on the graphic object to move.
2. Point anywhere on the graphic object.
3. Drag the graphic object to a new location.
4. Release the mouse button.

Graphic Object—Selecting

Before you can edit a graphic object, you must first select it. This can only be done with a mouse.

Mouse Steps

1. Position the mouse pointer over the object you want to select.

2. Click the mouse button, and selection handles will surround the object selected.

*To select multiple objects, press and hold the **Shift** key while selecting objects.*

TIP

Graphic Object—Sending to Back

Sends a graphic object to the back, behind all other objects. This requires a mouse.

Mouse Steps

1. Click on the object in the foreground.

2. Click on the Format menu.

3. Click on Send to Back.

TIP   *In place of steps 2 and 3, you can click the right mouse button to bring up the shortcut menu, and select **Send to Back**.*

Links—Creating

Links two or more worksheets together. When the source document is updated or changed, the linked documents will reflect the change. You can paste to the original worksheet, another Excel worksheet, or a different application.

Keyboard Steps

1. Open all the documents you want to link together.

2. Select the data you want to link (see **Selecting Cells**).

3. Using the Edit Copy command, insert data into the Clipboard.

4. Move to the worksheet or application you want to paste the link to.

TIP   *You can link to the same Excel document, another document, or another application altogether.*

5. Select the cell or insertion point you want to paste the Clipboard's contents to .... ↑ ↓ ← →
6. Select the Edit menu .... Alt + E
7. Select Paste Link L

Mouse Steps

1. Open all the documents you want to link together.

2. Select the data you want to link (see **Selecting Cells**).

3. Using the Edit Copy command, insert data into the Clipboard.

4. Move to the worksheet or application you want to paste the link to.

You can link to the same Excel document, another document, or another application altogether.
TIP

5. Click on the cell or insertion point you want to paste the Clipboard's contents to.

6. Click on the Edit menu.

7. Click on Paste Link.

Links—Creating

Links—Updating

Updates the values in the dependent linked document with those of the source document.

Keyboard Steps

1. Using the File Open command, open the document (dependent) that contains the linked reference.

2. Select File .... **Alt** + **F**

3. Select Links .... **L**

4. In the Links list box, select the source worksheet .... **↑** or **↓**

> **TIP** *You can select more than one source document in the Links list box by holding down the Ctrl key while selecting documents.*

5. To update the values in the dependent worksheet, select Update .... **Alt** + **U**

6. To open the selected worksheet, choose Open .... **Alt** + **O**

Mouse Steps

1. Using the **File Open** command, open the document (dependent) that contains the linked reference.
2. Click on **File**.
3. Click on **Links**.
4. In the Links list box, click on the source worksheet.

You can select more than one source document in the Links list box by holding down the Ctrl key while selecting documents.

5. To update the values in the dependent worksheet, click on Update.
6. To open the selected worksheet, click on Open.

Macro—Pausing Recording

*Pauses the recording of a macro. (To restart recording, see **Macro—Resuming Recording**.)*

Keyboard Steps

1. Select the Macro menu .... **Alt** + **M**
2. Select Stop Recorder .... **C**

Mouse Steps

1. Click on the **M**acro menu.
2. Click on Stop Re**c**order.

Macro—Recording

*Records frequently-used keystrokes or Excel commands, and saves them as a **macro**. If (for example) you enter your name or your company's name often, create a macro to write it for you with no mistakes. Then you can run the macro by pressing a couple of keys.*

Keyboard Steps

1. Select the **M**acro menu .... **Alt** + **M**
2. Select Re**c**ord .... **C**
3. In the **N**ame box, enter a
   name for the macro .... **Alt** + **N**

   name
4. In the **K**ey box, enter the
   shortcut keys .... **Alt** + **K**

   shortcut keys

EXAMPLE

*For example, **Ctrl+N** could be a shortcut for your company's name.*

5. In the Store Macro In box, select one of the following options:
   Global Macro Sheet .... `Alt` + `G`
   New Macro Sheet .... `Alt` + `M`
6. To begin recording, press .... `↵`
7. Perform the actions or keystrokes you want to record.
8. To stop recording, first select the Macro menu .... `Alt` + `M`
9. Select Stop Recorder .... `C`

*To run a macro, press the **Ctrl** key simultaneously with the shortcut key you assigned to the macro.*

TIP

Mouse Steps

1. Click on the Macro menu.
2. Click on Record.
3. Click in the Name box, and enter a name for the macro.
4. Click in the Key box, and enter the shortcut keys.

*For example, **Ctrl+N** could be a shortcut for your company's name.*

EXAMPLE

5. In the Store Macro In box, click on one of the following options:
   Global Macro Sheet
   New Macro Sheet

6. To begin recording, click on **OK**.

7. Perform the actions or keystrokes to record.

8. To stop recording, first click on the **M**acro menu.

9. Click on Stop Re**c**order.

*On the **Macro** toolbar, click on the **Macro Record** tool to record a macro, and the **Stop Recording** tool to stop recording.*

TIP

*To run a macro, press the **Ctrl** key simultaneously with the shortcut key you assigned to the macro.*

TIP

Macro—Resuming Recording

Resumes the recording of a macro that has been paused.

Macro—Recording

Keyboard Steps

1. Select the Macro menu .... `Alt` + `M`
2. Select Start Recorder .... `S`
3. Resume executing commands and keystrokes.

Mouse Steps

1. Click on the Macro menu.
2. Click on Start Recorder.
3. Resume executing commands and keystrokes.

Macro—Running

Performs the keystrokes or commands previously stored in a macro.

Keyboard Steps

1. Select the Macro menu .... `Alt` + `M`
2. Select **Run** .... `R`
3. From the **Run** list box, select a macro to run .... `Alt` + `R`
   `↑` or `↓`
4. To run the macro, press .... `↵`

To run a macro quickly, press the shortcut keys assigned to the macro during recording (for example, Ctrl+C).

Mouse Steps

1. Click on the **M**acro menu.
2. Click on **R**ecord.
3. From the **R**un list box, click on a macro to run.
4. To run the macro, click on **OK**.

To run a macro quickly, press the shortcut keys assigned to the macro during recording (for example, Ctrl+C).

Menu Commands—Selecting

Chooses commands from pull-down menus.

Keyboard Steps

1. To activate the menu bar, press and hold .... **Alt**
2. Type the underlined letter of the menu command .... ***underlined letter***

   OR

Macro—Running

Highlight the menu
command, using .... ← or →

Press .... ↵

3. Type the underlined letter
of the command .... *underlined letter*

   OR

   Highlight the command
   using .... ↑ or ↓

   Press .... ↵

Mouse Steps

1. Click on a command on the menu bar.
2. Click on a menu option.

Number—Formatting

Applies decimal, date, percent, currency, integers, or scientific notation formats to numbers in selected cells. To apply formatting quickly, choose a keyboard shortcut from the following table.

Press Ctrl+Shift+	Example Format
$	$#,##0.00 or $#,###.00
%	0.00%
!	0.00
#	d-mmm-yy
@	h:mm
^	0.00E+00

Number—Formatting 125

Keyboard Steps

1. Select the cells to which you want to apply the number formatting.

*To select the entire worksheet, press **Ctrl+Shift+Spacebar**.*

2. Select the Format menu .... `Alt` + `T`
3. Select Number .... `N`
4. In the Category list box,
   select a format category .... `Alt` + `C`
   `↑` or `↓`
5. In the Format Codes list box,
   select a format option .... `Alt` + `F`
   `↑` or `↓`

A sample of the format selected will appear in the sample area of the dialog box.

6. To apply the formatting, press .... `↵`

Mouse Steps

1. Select the cells to which you want to apply the number formatting.

126 Number—Formatting

To select the entire worksheet, click on the button at the intersection of the row and column headings in the top left corner of the worksheet.

2. Click on the Format menu.

3. Click on Number.

In place of steps 2 and 3, you can click the right mouse button to bring up the shortcut menu, and select Number.

4. In the **Category** list box, click on a format category.

5. In the **Format Codes** list box, click on a format option.

A sample of the format selected will appear in the sample area of the dialog box.

6. To apply the formatting, click on **OK**.

*To apply formatting quickly, click on the **Comma**, **Currency**, or **Percent** tools on the **Formatting** toolbar.*

Number—Formatting

OLE Object—Creating

Inserts an embedded object into an Excel worksheet. The kind of object you can insert depends on the applications loaded on your system. (The steps for inserting objects may vary slightly from those listed here, due to differences in applications. See the application's documentation if you have problems.)

Keyboard Steps

1. Select the Edit menu .... Alt + E
2. Select Insert Object .... O
3. In the Object Type list, select the object you want to insert .... Alt + O
   ↑ or ↓
4. To insert the object, press .... ↵

Depending on the object you are inserting, more steps may be needed to create the object. For example, if you are inserting a drawn object, you'll need to draw it first.

TIP

5. When you're finished creating the object, choose File .... Alt + F
6. Choose Exit & Return to Sheet X

Note that for some applications, you'll simply have to choose OK rather than using steps 5 and 6.

Mouse Steps

1. Click on the Edit menu.
2. Click on Insert Object.
3. In the Object Type list, click on the object you want to insert.
4. To insert the object, click on **OK**.

Depending on the object you are inserting, more steps may be needed to create the object. For example, to insert a drawn object, you'll need to draw it first.

5. When you're finished creating the object, click on **File**.
6. Click on Exit & Return to Sheet.

Note that for some applications, you'll simply have to choose OK rather than using steps 5 and 6.

OLE Object—Editing

*Edits an object that has been embedded into an Excel document (worksheet). (To move the embedded object, see **Graphic Object—Moving**.)*

Mouse Steps

1. Position the mouse pointer over the object you want to select.
2. Double-click on the object.
3. Edit the object in the software program as necessary.
4. Exit the program to return to Excel.

OLE Object—Selecting

Selects an embedded object on the worksheet. This requires a mouse.

Mouse Steps

1. Position the mouse pointer over the object you want to select.
2. Click the mouse button and selection handles will surround the object selected.

*To select multiple objects, press and hold the **Shift** key while selecting objects.*

Outline—Creating

Create an outline from data in a range or worksheet.

Keyboard Steps

1. Select a range to outline.

   TIP *To outline the entire worksheet, select only one cell in the worksheet.*

2. Select the Formula menu .... Alt + R
3. Select Outline .... O
4. To apply built-in outlining styles, select the Automatic Styles check box .... Alt + A
5. Select the direction of the levels in the outline:
   Summary rows below detail .... Alt + B
   Summary columns to right of detail .... Alt + R
6. Select Create .... Alt + C

Mouse Steps

1. Select a range to outline.

To outline the entire worksheet, select only one cell in the worksheet.

2. Click on the Formula menu.
3. Click on Outline.
4. To apply built-in outlining styles, click on the Automatic Styles check box.
5. Click on the direction of the levels in the outline:
   Summary rows below detail
   Summary columns to right of detail
6. Click on Create.

Page Breaks—Automatic

Turn on this feature so that Excel determines the location of a page break automatically, and inserts a dashed line to indicate the break.

Keyboard Steps

1. Select the Options menu .... `Alt` + `O`
2. Select Display .... `D`
3. Select Automatic Page Breaks .... `B`
4. Press .... `⏎`

Outline—Creating

Mouse Steps

1. Click on the **Options** menu.
2. Click on **Display**.
3. Click on the Automatic Page **Breaks** check box.
4. Click on **OK**.

Page Breaks—Manual—Adding

Inserts a manual page break (either horizontal or vertical), displays it with a dashed line, and adjusts any following page breaks automatically.

Keyboard Steps

1. Select the cell below and/or to the right of where you want to insert the page break.
2. Select the Options menu .... `Alt` + `O`
3. Select Set Page Break .... `B`

Mouse Steps

1. Select the cell below and/or to the right of where you want to insert the page break.
2. Click on the **Options** menu.
3. Click on Set Page **Break**.

Page Breaks—Manual—Deleting

Deletes manual page breaks, either horizontal or vertical.

Keyboard Steps

1. Select the cell immediately below or to the right of the page break (dashed line).

   *If you want to remove all page breaks, press **Ctrl+Shift+Spacebar** to select the entire document.*

2. Select the Options menu .... `Alt` + `O`
3. Select Remove Page Break .... `B`

Mouse Steps

1. Select the cell immediately below or to the right of the page break (dashed line).

   If you want to remove all page breaks, select the entire document by clicking on the button in the top left corner, at the intersection of the row and column headings.

2. Click on the Options menu.
3. Click on Remove Page Break.

Printing—Document

Prints or previews the active document. Select any options in the Print dialog box (listed in the table that follows).

Option	Description
All	Prints entire document.
Pages	Determines what pages to print.
Print Quality	Determines the resolution quality of the selected printer.
Copies	Determines how many copies of the document to print.
Sheet	Prints only the worksheet.
Notes	Prints only worksheet notes.
Both	Prints both worksheet and notes.
Preview	Previews the document on the screen as it will be printed on paper.
Fast, But no	Prints everything quickly except graphics.
Page Setup	Sets how a document will look when printed.

TIP *To print only a portion of the worksheet, use the Options Set Print Area command (see **Printing—Setting Print Area**).*

Keyboard Steps

1. In the active window, display the document to print.
2. Select the File menu .... `Alt` + `F`
3. Select Print .... `P`
4. Select any of the options listed in the preceding table .... `Alt` + *selection letter*
5. When ready to print, press .... `↵`

TIP *To print quickly, press **Ctrl+Shift+F12** or **Alt+Ctrl+Shift+F2**.*

Mouse Steps

1. In the active window, display the document to print.
2. Click on the File menu.
3. Click on Print.
4. Click on any of the options listed in the previous table.

5. When ready to print, click on **OK**.

*To print quickly, click on the **Print** tool in the **Standard** toolbar.*

Printing—Page Setup

Option	Description
Portrait	Prints a document using the short sides of the paper as top and bottom.
Landscape	Prints a document using the long sides of the paper as top and bottom.
Size	Lists different paper sizes in a drop-down list.
Margins	Sets **L**eft, **R**ight, **T**op and **B**ottom margins.
Center Horizontally	Centers a document between top and bottom margins.
Center Vertically	Centers a document between left and right margins.

continues

continued

Option	Description
Row & Column Headings	Prints row and column headings on the worksheet.
Cell Gridlines	Prints the cell gridlines on paper.
Black & White Cells	Prints colored cells in a pattern unless the box is left blank (in which case, they are printed in black and white).
Start Page No.'s At	Starts printing at the page number specified.
Down then Over	Prints a page from top to bottom, and then right.
Over then Down	Prints a page from left to right, and then down.
Fit To	Compresses the document to fit in the specified page layout.
Reduce/Enlarge to	Reduces or enlarges the document by percentage.
Options Button	Sets or removes page breaks.

Option	Description
Header	Adds a header to print at the top of each page.
Footer	Adds a footer to print at the bottom of each page.
Print	Prints the document.
Printer Setup	Allows you to change the printer setup or select another printer.

Keyboard Steps

1. Select the File menu .... `Alt` + `F`
2. Select Page Setup .... `T`
3. Select any option listed in the previous table .... `Alt` + *selection letter*
4. When finished, press .... `↵`

Mouse Steps

1. Click on the File menu.
2. Click on Page Setup.
3. Click on any of the options listed in the table above.
4. When finished, click on **OK**.

Printing—Print Preview

Displays the document on-screen as it will appear when printed on paper. The table that follows lists the Preview options.

You can't edit a document while previewing it.

TIP

Option	Description
Next	Displays the next page of the document.
Previous	Displays the previous page of the document.
Zoom	Toggles between full-page and actual-size views.
Print	Displays the Print dialog box to print the document.
Setup	Displays the Page Setup dialog box.
Margins	Allows you to adjust the margins of the document by dragging the margin markers.
Close	Closes the preview window and returns to the document.

Keyboard Steps

1. In the active window, display the document to print.

2. Select the File menu .... Alt + F
3. Select Preview V
4. Select any option listed in the previous table .... Alt + *selection letter*
5. When finished previewing, press .... Alt + C

Mouse Steps

1. In the active window, display the document to print.
2. Click on the File menu.
3. Click on Preview.
4. Click on any option listed in the previous table.
5. When finished previewing, click on Close.

*To preview a document quickly, click on the **Preview** tool found on the **Custom** toolbar.*

TIP

Printing—Removing Print Area

Removes the specified print area of the worksheet.

Keyboard Steps

1. Select the entire worksheet .... [Ctrl] + [Shift] + [Space]
2. Select the Options menu .... [Alt] + [O]
3. Select Remove Print Area .... [A]

Mouse Steps

1. Select the entire worksheet by clicking on the button at the intersection of the row and column headings.
2. Click on the Options menu.
3. Click on Remove Print Area.

Printing—Removing Print Titles

Removes titles from the worksheet that were set to print on each page.

Keyboard Steps

1. Select the entire worksheet .... [Ctrl] + [Shift] + [Space]
2. Select the Options menu .... [Alt] + [O]
3. Select Remove Print Titles .... [T]

Mouse Steps

1. Select the entire worksheet by clicking on the button at the intersection of the row and column headings.
2. Click on the **Options** menu.
3. Click on **Remove Print Titles**.

Printing—Setting Print Area

*Sets a specified area of the worksheet to be printed. (To delete a print area, see **Printing—Removing Print Area**.)*

Keyboard Steps

1. Select the cells to be printed.
2. Select the Options menu .... `Alt` + `O`
3. Select Set Print Area .... `A`

Mouse Steps

1. Select the cells to be printed.
2. Click on the **Options** menu.
3. Click on Set Print Area.

Printing—Setting Print Titles

Sets specified rows and column text as titles to be printed on each page of the worksheet.

Keyboard Steps

1. Select the entire row or column containing the titles to print on each page (see **Selecting Cells**).

2. Select the Options menu .... `Alt` + `O`

3. Select Set Print Titles .... `T`

Mouse Steps

1. Select the entire row or column containing the titles to print on each page (see **Selecting Cells**).

2. Click on the Options menu.

3. Click on Set Print Titles.

Range—Applying Names

Searches the selected cells in a range for formulas, and replaces the cell range references with range names.

Keyboard Steps

1. Select the range whose cell references you want to replace with range names.

2. Select the Formula menu .... `Alt` + `R`

3. Select **A**pply Names .... `A`

4. In the Apply **N**ames list box,
   select a name to apply .... `Alt` + `N`
   `↑` or `↓`

5. **(Optional)** To replace all
   cell references (whether
   relative or absolute), select
   the **I**gnore Relative/Absolute
   check box... `Alt` + `I`

6. **(Optional)** To replace the
   cell reference with row
   and column names, select
   the Use Row and Column
   Names check box.............................. `Alt` + `U`

7. To apply the selected name,
   press .... `↵`

Mouse Steps

1. Select the range whose cell references you want to replace with range names.

2. Click on the Formula menu.

3. Click on Apply Names.

4. In the Apply Names list box, click on a name to apply.

5. **(Optional)** To replace all cell references (whether relative or absolute), select the **I**gnore Relative/Absolute check box.

6. **(Optional)** To replace the cell reference with row and column names, select the Use Row and Column Names check box.

7. To apply the selected name, click on **OK**.

Range—Defining Names

Defines a name for the selected cell range. This name can then be used to refer to the cell range in formulas. Names are generally easier to read in formulas than in cell addresses.

Keyboard Steps

1. Select the range to name.
2. Select the Formula menu .... `Alt` + `R`
3. Select **D**efine Name .... `D`

> **TIP** *To define a name quickly, press Ctrl+F3.*

4. In the **N**ame box, enter a
   range name .... `Alt` + `N`
   range name

5. To add the name, select the
   Add button .... `Alt` + `A`

6. Press .... `↵`

Mouse Steps

1. Select the range to name.
2. Click on the Formula menu.
3. Click on **Define Name**.
4. In the **Name** box, enter a range name.
5. To add the name, click on the **Add** button.
6. Click on **OK**.

Range—Deleting Names

Deletes a range name from the range name list.

Keyboard Steps

1. Select the Formula menu .... `Alt` + `R`
2. Select **Define Name** .... `D`

To define a name quickly, press Ctrl+F3.

TIP

3. In the Names in Sheet list box, select the range name to delete .... `Alt` + `S`

   `↑` or `↓`
4. Select Delete .... `Alt` + `D`
5. To delete the range name, press .... `↵`

Mouse Steps

1. Click on the Formula menu.
2. Click on **Define Name**.
3. In the Names in Sheet list box, click on the range name to delete.
4. Click on **Delete**.
5. To delete the range name, click on **OK**.

Range—Editing Names

Edits or changes the defined range names.

Keyboard Steps

1. Select the range with the name to edit.
2. Select the Formula menu .... **Alt** + **R**
3. Select **Define Name** .... **D**

To define a name quickly, press Ctrl+F3.

4. (Optional) In the Name box, edit the range name .... **Alt** + **N**
   range name

5. (Optional) In the Refers To box, edit the range .... **Alt** + **R**

6. To save the edits, press .... [↵]

Mouse Steps

1. Select the range with the range name to edit.
2. Click on the Formula menu.
3. Click on **Define** Name.
4. **(Optional)** In the **N**ame box, edit the range name.
5. **(Optional)** In the **R**efers To box, edit the range address.
6. To save the edits, click on **OK**.

Range—Filling Cells Down

Fills the contents in the selected cells below the top cell with the top cell's contents and formats.

Keyboard Steps

1. Select a range of cells including the top cell which contains the data to be copied.
2. Select the Edit menu .... [Alt] + [E]
3. Select Fill Down .... [W]

*To fill down quickly, press **Ctrl+D** or **Ctrl+<**.*

Mouse Steps

1. Select a range of cells including the top cell which contains the data to be copied.
2. Click on the Edit menu.
3. Click on Fill Down.

To fill down by dragging, select the cell(s) you want to copy down. Point to the handle at the lower right corner of the cell, so that the mouse pointer turns into a small plus sign (+). Drag so the border outlines all the cells you want to copy to, then release the mouse button. (If you're copying formulas with relative references, Excel will adjust those references in the formula copies.)

Range—Filling Cells Right

Fills the selected cells to the right of the far-left selected cell with its contents and formats.

To fill right by dragging, select the cell(s) you want to copy right. Point to the handle at the lower right corner of the cell, so that the mouse

*pointer turns into a small plus sign (+). Drag
so the border outlines all the cells you want to
copy to, then release the mouse button. (If
you're copying formulas with relative references, Excel will adjust those references in the
formula copies.)*

Keyboard Steps

1. Select a range of cells,
   including the far-left cell
   which contains the data
   to be copied.
2. Select the Edit menu .... Alt + E
3. Select Fill Right .... H

*To fill right quickly, press Ctrl+R or
Ctrl+>.*

TIP

Mouse Steps

1. Select a range of cells including the far-left cell
   which contains the data to be copied.
2. Click on the Edit menu.
3. Click on Fill Right.

Range—Filling Cells Right

Range—Filling with Series

Fills a range of selected cells with a series of numbers or dates, incrementing the data automatically as you specify.

EXAMPLE *For example, you can use this command to number cells going down a column (as 1, 2, 3, 4, etc.), or dates (as 01/01, 01/02, 01/03, etc.).*

Keyboard Steps

1. Enter a number or date in the cell where the series is to begin.

2. Select the cells to be filled, including the cell with the number or date.

3. Select the **D**ata menu .... `Alt` + `D`
4. Select Se**r**ies .... `R`
5. In the **T**ype box, select one of the following options:
   Linear .... `Alt` + `L`
   Growth .... `Alt` + `G`
   Date .... `Alt` + `D`
   AutoFill .... `Alt` + `F`

6. If you chose **D**ate in the Type box, select one of the following options in the Date **U**nit box:
   Day .... `Alt` + `A`
   Weekday .... `Alt` + `W`
   Month .... `Alt` + `M`
   Year .... `Alt` + `Y`

7. In the **S**tep value box, enter a number to increment the set by .... `Alt` + `S`
   ####

If you enter a negative number, it will decrease the values in the series.

TIP

8. (**Optional**) Display the St**o**p Value text box .... `Alt` + `O`
   Enter a value to stop at .... *####*

9. (**Optional**) Select **T**rend to create a linear or exponential growth trend .... `Alt` + `T`

10. When finished, press .... `↵`

Mouse Steps

1. Enter a number or date in the cell where the series is to begin.

Range—Filling with Series

2. Select the cells to be filled, including the cell with the number or date.

3. Click on the **Data** menu.

4. Click on Series.

5. In the **Type** box, click on one of the following options:
   Linear
   Growth
   Date
   AutoFill

6. If you chose **Date** in the **Type** box, click on one of the following options in the Date Unit box:
   Day
   Weekday
   Month
   Year

7. In the **Step** value box, enter a number to increment the data by.

If you enter a negative number, it will decrease the values in the series.

8. **(Optional)** In the Stop Value text box, enter a value to stop at.

9. **(Optional)** Click on Trend to create a linear or exponential growth trend.

10. When finished, click on **OK**.

Repeating—Operations and Commands

Repeats an Excel command or operation.

EXAMPLE

*Excel can't repeat all operations and commands. In that case, the message **Can't Repeat** will appear on the Edit menu.*

Keyboard Steps

1. Perform the Excel command or operation you want to repeat.
2. Select the Edit menu .... **Alt** + **E**
3. Select **R**epeat .... **R**

TIP

*To repeat an operation or command quickly, press **Alt+Enter**.*

Mouse Steps

1. Perform the Excel command or operation you want to repeat.
2. Click on the Edit menu.
3. Click on **R**epeat.

Repeating—Operations and Commands 155

Row—Changing Height

Changes the height of the selected row(s).

Keyboard Steps

1. Select a cell(s) from any row to change the height.

   *To change the row height on the entire worksheet, press **Ctrl+Shift+Spacebar**.*

2. Select the Format menu .... `Alt` + `T`
3. Select Row Height .... `R`
4. In the Row Height text box, enter a row height .... `####`

   *Measure row height in **points**; 72 points = 1 inch.*

5. **(Optional)** To use the standard row height, select the Use Standard Height check box .... `Alt` + `S`

6. **(Optional)** Select Hide to set the row height to zero, and to hide the row on the worksheet .... `Alt` + `I`

7. When finished setting row height, press .... `↵`

Mouse Steps

1. Point to the bottom border (line) of the row to change.

2. Click and drag the line to a desired size.

3. Release the mouse button.

Row—Deleting

See **Cell—Deleting**.

Row—Inserting

See **Cell—Inserting**.

Selecting Cells

Selects a cell(s) in a worksheet. Before most Excel commands can be executed, a cell or range of cells must first be selected to perform the operation.

Keyboard Steps

To Select	Press
A single cell	`↑` `↓` `←` `→`
Range of cells	`Shift` + `↑` `↓` `←` `→`
Entire row	`Shift` + `Space`
Entire column	`Ctrl` + `Space`
All cells in worksheet	`Ctrl` + `Alt` + `Space`
Deselect a cell	`↑` `↓` `←` `→`

Mouse Steps

To Select	Click on
A single cell	The cell.
Range of cells	The cell, and drag over the range.
Entire row	The row heading.
Entire column	The column heading.
All cells in worksheet	The button at intersection of the row and column headings.
Deselect a cell	Any other cell.

Selecting—Multiple Ranges of Cells

Select multiple cells, cell ranges, rows or columns in a worksheet.

Keyboard Steps

1. Select the first cell, range, row, or column.
2. Press .... Shift + F8
3. Outline cells to select .... ↑ ↓ ← →
4. Press F8
5. Press .... Shift + F8
6. Repeat steps 3–5 to select other cells.

Mouse Steps

1. Select the first cell, range, row, or column.
2. Press and hold the Ctrl key.
3. Click or drag the mouse over the other cells to select.
4. Release the Ctrl key and mouse button.

Selecting—Special Data

Searches for and selects cells that meet specified criteria.

For example, if you were searching for a special note, you could use the Select Special command to search for all cells with notes attached.

Keyboard Steps

1. Select the range of cells to search.

To search the entire document, do not select a range.

2. Select the Formula menu .... Alt + R
3. Select Select Special .... S
4. Select an option to search .... Alt + *selection letter*
5. When finished, press .... ↵

Mouse Steps

1. Select the range of cells to search.

To search the entire document, do not select a range.

2. Click on the Formula menu.
3. Click on Select Special.

Selecting—Special Data

4. Click on any of the options to search.

5. When finished, click on **OK**.

Shortcut Menu

Excel offers shortcut menus which display the most common Excel commands used with the selected item, saving you the trouble of searching for a command in the pull-down menus.

Keyboard Steps

1. Select the desired cell(s) or object.

2. Press .... `Shift` + `F10`

3. Select a shortcut menu option .... `↑` or `↓`

4. Press .... `↵`

Mouse Steps

1. Select the desired cell(s) or object.

2. Click the right mouse button.

3. Click on a shortcut menu option.

Spelling—Checking

Checks all of your spelling within the document for misspelled or unrecognized words, and offers suggestions.

Command Button	Description
Ignore	Ignores the word and leaves it unchanged.
Ignore All	Ignores every occurrence of the word.
Change	Replaces the current word with the word in the Change To box.
Change All	Replaces every occurrence of the word with the word in the Change To box.
Add	Adds the word to the dictionary.
Cancel or Close	Closes the Spellings dialog box.
Suggest	Displays a list of suggested words if the Always Suggest check box is not checked.
Ignore Words in UPPERCASE	Ignores all word in uppercase.
Always Suggest	Always suggests a word.

Keyboard Steps

1. Select the Options menu .... `Alt` + `O`
2. Select Spelling .... `S`

3. When a misspelled word appears in the Not in Dictionary box, a suggested replacement appears in the Change To box, and other replacement words appear in the Suggestions box. If suggestions do not appear, select the Suggest button by pressing .... **Alt** + **S**

4. To correct the spelling, select one of the command buttons listed in the previous table by pressing .... **Alt** + *selection letter*

5. Press .... **⏎**

Mouse Steps

1. Click on the Options menu.

2. Click on Spelling.

3. When a misspelled word appears in the Not in Dictionary box, a suggested replacement appears in the Change To box, and other replacement words appear in the Suggestions box. If a suggestion does not appear, click on the Suggest button.

4. To correct the spelling, click on one of the command buttons listed in the previous table.

*To check the spelling in your document quickly, click on the **Spelling** tool in the **Utility** toolbar.*

Toolbars—Selecting Tool

Selects a tool from an Excel toolbar.

A mouse is required to select a tool from a toolbar.

You can move a toolbar to a different portion of the screen by clicking anywhere on it and dragging it to a new location. Sizing a toolbar is similar to sizing any window: click on a border and drag to a new size.

Mouse Steps

1. Select the desired cell(s) to change.
2. Click on the desired tool from a toolbar.

Toolbar—Showing and Hiding

Displays or hides a toolbar on the document.

Keyboard Steps

1. Select the Options menu .... `Alt` + `O`

2. Select Toolbars .... `O`

3. From the Show Toolbar
   list box, select a toolbar
   to show or hide .... `↑` or `↓`

4. To display the toolbar,
   select Show .... `Alt` + `S`

   OR

   To remove the toolbar,
   select Hide .... `Alt` + `I`

Mouse Steps

1. Point to any toolbar displayed in the document.

2. Click the right mouse button.

3. Click on the name of the toolbar you want to show or hide.

Toolbar—Tool Description

Shows a description of the tool's purpose in the status bar.

A mouse is required to display a tool's description.

Mouse Steps

1. Point to a tool on a toolbar.
2. Click and hold the left mouse button.
3. A description of the tool will appear on the status bar.
4. To use the tool, release the mouse button.
5. To cancel the tool, drag the pointer to any location outside of the toolbar and release the mouse button.

Undo—Commands and Operations

Reverses an Excel command or operation if you made a mistake or did not like the previous results. (For best results, use Undo before executing your next command.)

Keyboard Steps

1. Select the Edit menu .... **Alt** + **E**
2. Select Undo .... **U**

*To undo a command quickly, press **Alt+Backspace** or **Ctrl+Z**.*

Mouse Steps

1. Click on the Edit menu.
2. Click on Undo.

Window—Activating

Activates an open window by selecting it and placing the cell selector in it.

Keyboard Steps

1. Select the Window menu .... Alt + W
2. Type the number which appears to the left of the window you want to activate .... #

Mouse Steps

1. Click on the Window menu.
2. Click on the document name.

You can click anywhere on the visible portion of a window to activate it.

Window—Arranging

Rearranges windows on the screen.

Keyboard Steps

1. Select the Window menu .... `Alt` + `W`
2. Select Arrange .... `A`
3. In the Arrange box, select an option:
   Tiled .... `Alt` + `T`
   Horizontal .... `Alt` + `O`
   Vertical .... `Alt` + `V`
   None .... `Alt` + `N`
4. Press .... `↵`

Mouse Steps

1. Click on the Window menu.
2. Click on **Arrange**.
3. Click on an option from the Arrange box:
   Tiled
   Horizontal
   Vertical
   None
4. Click on **OK**.

Window—Arranging Icons

Arranges all minimized window icons on the bottom of the screen.

Keyboard Steps

1. Select the Windows menu .... `Alt` + `W`
2. Select Arrange Icons .... `A`

Mouse Steps

1. Click on the Window menu.
2. Click on **Arrange Icons**.

Window—Closing Window

Closes the active document window.

Keyboard Steps

1. Select the document's
   Control menu .... `Alt` + `-`
2. Select Close .... `C`

*To close a document window quickly, press **Ctrl+F4**.*

Mouse Steps

1. Click on the document's Control menu box (in the upper left corner of the window).

2. Click on Close.

*To close a document window quickly, double-click on the document's **Control menu** box.*

Window—Freezing and Unfreezing

Stops scrolling of the top and left panes of a split window.

Keyboard Steps

1. Select the Window menu.

2. Select Freeze Panes .... **F**

   OR

   Select Unfreeze Panes .... **F**

Mouse Steps

1. Click on the Window menu.

2. Click on Freeze Panes or Unfreeze Panes.

*To freeze a pane quickly, you can click on the **Freeze Pane** tool from the **Custom** toolbar.*

Window—Hiding and Unhiding

Hides the active window from view without closing it.

Keyboard Steps

1. Select the Window menu .... `Alt` + `W`
2. Select Hide .... `H`

*To unhide a window, select Unhide from the **Window** menu by pressing U, selecting the hidden window from the list, and pressing **Enter**.*

Mouse Steps

1. Click on the Window menu.
2. Click on Hide.

*To unhide a window, click on Unhide from the **Window** menu, click on the hidden window from the list, and click on **OK**.*

Window—Maximizing Window

Expands a document (worksheet) window to fill the entire screen.

Keyboard Steps

1. Select the document's Control menu .... **Alt** + **-**
2. Select Maximize .... **X**

*To maximize a document window quickly, press **Ctrl+F10**.*

*To restore the window to the previous size, press **Alt+–** to display the document's Control menu, and then select **Restore** or press **Ctrl+F5**.*

Mouse Steps

1. Click on the document's Control menu box in the upper left corner of the window.
2. Click on Maximize.

*To maximize a document window quickly, click on the **Maximize** icon in the upper right corner of the document window, or double-click on the window's **title bar**.*

*TIP — To restore the window to the previous size, click on the **Restore** icon in the upper right corner of the document window.*

Window—Minimizing Window

Collapses the document window to an icon at the bottom of the screen.

Keyboard Steps

1. Select the document's
   Control menu .... Alt + -
2. Select Minimize .... N

*TIP — To minimize a document window quickly, press **Ctrl+F9**.*

*TIP — To restore the window to the previous size, press **Alt+-** to display the document's Control menu, and then select Restore or press **Ctrl+F5**.*

Mouse Steps

1. Click on the document's Control menu box in the upper left corner of the window.
2. Click on Minimize.

*To minimize a document window quickly, click on the **Minimize** icon in the upper right corner of the document window.*

*To restore a document window to its previous size, click on the **Restore** icon in the upper right corner of the document window.*

Window—Moving Window

Moves the document window to a new location. (Note that you can't move a maximized window.)

Keyboard Steps

1. Select the document's Control menu .... **Alt** + **-**
2. Select Move .... **M**
3. Move the window to a new location .... **↑** **↓** **←** **→**
4. When the window is in the new location, press .... **↵**

*To move a document window quickly, press **Ctrl+F7**.*

Mouse Steps

1. Point to the document's title bar.
2. Press the left mouse button and drag to a new location.

Window—New Window

Creates a new window of the active document, so you can display different portions of the document at the same time.

Any changes you make to one window will affect the other, but the windows won't scroll together.

Keyboard Steps

1. Select the Window menu .... Alt + W
2. Select New Window .... N

Mouse Steps

1. Click on the Window menu.
2. Click on New Window.

Window—Next Window

Switches between open document windows.

Keyboard Steps

1. Select the document's
   Control menu .... `Alt` + `-`
2. Select Next Window .... `T`

> *To switch to the next document window quickly, press **Ctrl+F6**.*
>
> **TIP**

Mouse Steps

1. Click on the document's Control menu box in the upper left corner of the window.
2. Click on Next Window.

Window—Restoring Window

*See **Window—Maximizing Window** or **Window—Minimizing Window**.*

Window—Sizing Window

Changes the size of the document window.

Keyboard Steps

1. Select the document's
   Control menu .... `Alt` + `-`
2. Select Size .... `S`

3. Size the window, using .... ↑ ↓ ← →

4. After the window is sized,
   press .... ↵

> *To size a document window quickly, press **Ctrl+F8**.*

Mouse Steps

1. Point to the document's window border and the mouse pointer will change to a two-headed arrow.

2. Press the left mouse button and drag the pointer to the desired size.

Window—Splitting Window

Splits a document window into panes so you can see different portions of the document simultaneously.

Keyboard Steps

1. Select the document's
   Control menu .... Alt + -

2. Select Split .... P

3. Move the pointer to where
   you want to split the
   window .... ↑ ↓ ← →

4. Press .... ⏎

> TIP: *To unsplit a window, select Remove Split from the Window menu.*

Mouse Steps

1. Click on the split bars (solid black rectangles found in the window's bottom left and top right corners).

2. Drag to where you want to split the window.

> TIP: *To remove a split, click on Remove Split from the Window menu.*

Window—Zooming

Magnifies the display of the active window.

Keyboard Steps

1. Select the Window menu .... Alt + W
2. Select Zoom .... Z
3. Select one of the following magnifications:
   200 .... Alt + 0
   100 .... Alt + 1

75 .... Alt + 7
50 .... Alt + 5
25 .... Alt + 2

4. **(Optional)** Select Fit Selection to magnify only the selected range .... Alt + F

5. **(Optional)** Select Custom to enter a magnification of your choice .... Alt + C
   Enter a magnification value .... ###

6. Press .... ↵

Mouse Steps

1. Click on the Window menu.

2. Click on Zoom.

3. Click on one of the following magnifications:
   200
   100
   75
   50
   25

4. **(Optional)** Click on Fit Selection to magnify only the selected range.

5. **(Optional)** Click on Custom to enter a magnification of your choice; enter a magnification value.

6. Click on OK.

Workbook—Adding Existing Documents

Adds existing documents (worksheets) to the workbook.

Keyboard Steps

1. From the workbook's contents window, select the **A**dd button .... `Alt` + `Shift` + `A`

2. Select **O**pen .... `Alt` + `O`

3. In the **File** list box, select a file to add .... `Tab`
   `↑` or `↓`

*If you need to change to another directory, press **Alt+D** to select the **Directories** list box, and select a directory. To select a different drive, press **Alt+V** to select the Drives list box, and select a drive.*

4. Press .... `↵`

5. Repeat steps 2–5 to add any new documents.

6. When finished adding new documents, select Close .... `Esc`

Mouse Steps

1. From the workbook contents window, click on the Add button.

2. Click on Open.

3. In the File list box, click on a file to add.

If you need to change to another directory, click on the Directories list box and select a directory. To select a different drive, click on the Drives list box and select a drive.

4. Click on **OK**.

5. Repeat steps 2–5 to add any new documents.

6. When finished adding new documents, click on Close.

Workbook—Adding New Documents

Adds new documents (worksheets) to the workbook.

Keyboard Steps

1. From the workbook's contents window, select the Add button .... **Alt** + **Shift** + **A**

2. Select New .... **Alt** + **N**

3. In the New list box, select a document type .... `Alt` + `N`
   `↑` or `↓`

4. Press .... `↵`

5. Repeat steps 2–5 to add any new documents.

6. When finished adding new documents, select .... `Esc`

Mouse Steps

1. From the workbook's contents window, click on the Add button.

2. Click on New.

3. In the New list box, click on a document type.

4. Click on OK.

5. Repeat steps 2–5 to add any new documents.

6. When finished adding new documents, click on Close.

Workbook—Creating

*Creates a **workbook**—an area where all materials related to a task (charts, worksheets, macros, etc.) are stored.*

Workbook—Adding New Documents

EXAMPLE *You could create a workbook if you are working on a presentation that requires many related worksheets and charts. The workbook would contain these related files; they would open automatically when the workbook is opened.*

Keyboard Steps

1. Select the File menu .... `Alt` + `F`
2. Select New .... `N`
3. In the New list box, select Workbook .... `↑` or `↓`
4. To create the workbook, press .... `↵`

Mouse Steps

1. Click on the File menu.
2. Click on New.
3. In the New list box, click on Workbook.
4. To create the workbook, click on **OK**.

Workbook—Opening a Document

Opens and displays a document (worksheet) from the workbook into the active window.

Keyboard Steps

1. From the workbook's contents window, highlight the document you want to open .... ↑ or ↓
2. Press .... ↵

Mouse Steps

1. From the workbook's contents window, point to the document you want to open.
2. Double-click on the document icon.

Workbook—Removing Documents

Removes a document (worksheet) from the workbook.

Keyboard Steps

1. From the workbook's contents window, select a document to remove .... ↑ or ↓
2. To remove, press .... Alt + Shift + R

Mouse Steps

1. From the workbook's contents window, point to a document to remove.
2. Drag the document onto the Excel workspace.
3. Release the mouse button.

Workbook—Saving

Saves a workbook file and all of its documents.

Keyboard Steps

1. Select the File menu .... `Alt` + `F`
2. Select Save Workbook .... `W`
3. In the File Name text box, enter a name for the workbook .... ***name***

> **TIP** *If you need to change to another directory, press **Alt+D** to select the Directories list box, and select a directory. To select a different drive, press **Alt+V** to select the Drives list box, and select a drive.*

4. To save the workbook, press .... `↵`

Mouse Steps

1. Click on the File menu.
2. Click on Save Workbook.
3. In the File Name text box, enter a name for the workbook.

*If you need to change to another directory, click on the **Directories** list box and select a directory. To select a different drive, click on the **Drives** list box and select a drive.*

4. To save the workbook, click on **OK**.

Worksheet—Grouping and Ungrouping

Grouping worksheets allows them to be edited and updated together, as a group.

Keyboard Steps

1. Select the **Options** menu .... **Alt** + **O**
2. Select Group Edit .... **G**
3. Select the worksheets to group .... **↑** or **↓**

*To select contiguous worksheets, press the **Shift** key while selecting files. To select non-contiguous worksheets, press the **Ctrl** key while selecting files.*

To ungroup, select the worksheet to remove from the group.

4. When finished selecting worksheets, press ....

Mouse Steps

1. Click on the Options menu.
2. Click on Group Edit.
3. Click on the worksheets to group.

*To select contiguous worksheets, press the **Shift** key while clicking on files. To select non-contiguous worksheets, press the **Ctrl** key while clicking on files.*

To ungroup, click on the worksheet to remove from the group.

4. When finished selecting worksheets, click on **OK**.

Workspace—Setting Options

Sets workspace options which apply to all documents. The options are listed in the following table.

Option	Description
Fixed Decimal Places	Sets decimal places. Enter a number of decimal places.

continues

continued

Option	Description
R1C1	Changes cell references from A1 to R1C1.
Status Bar	Displays the status bar.
Info Window	Displays info window.
Scroll Bars	Displays scroll bars.
Formula Bar	Displays the formula bar.
Note Indicator	Indicates a cell note in a cell with a dot in the top right corner of cell.
Alternate Menu or Help Key	Sets another menu or Help key which duplicates the Alt key.
Microsoft Excel Menus	Displays Excel menu help.
Lotus 1-2-3 Help	Displays Lotus 1-2-3 Help.
Alternate Navigation Keys	Uses a different set of keystrokes to navigate Excel.
Ignore Remote Requests	Ignores other Windows applications.
Move Selection after Enter	Moves the active cell down one row when the Enter key is pressed.

Option
Cell **D**rag and Drop

Description
Turns the drag-and-drop feature on and off.

Keyboard Steps

1. Select the **O**ptions menu .... `Alt` + `O`
2. Select **W**orkspace .... `W`
3. Select any option listed in the previous table .... `Alt` + *selection letter*
4. To save workspace settings, press .... `⏎`

Mouse Steps

1. Click on the **O**ptions menu.
2. Click on **W**orkspace.
3. Click on any option listed in the previous table.
4. To save workspace settings, click on **OK**.

Appendix A

Common Excel Functions

Function	Description	Example
ABS*(number)*	Calculates a number's absolute value	ABS(-2)
AVERAGE*(range)*	Calculates a number's average range	AVERAGE(A1:C12)
CHAR*(number)*	Finds the ANSI character for the number	CHAR(33)
CODE*(text)*	Finds the ANSI code for 1st character in specified text	CODE("Apple")
COUNT*(range)*	Counts number of cells in a range	COUNT(A1:W40)
COUNTA*(range)*	Counts number of non-blank cells in a range	COUNTA(A1:C15)
DATE*(date)*	Calculates the date number of a date	DATE("93,1,1")
DATEVALUE*(text)*	Converts a date into a number	DATEVALUE("01/01/94")
DAY*(date)*	Returns the day of the month within the date	DAY("04/31/93")

continues

continued

Function	Description	Example
DDB*(cost,salvage, life, period,factor)*	Calculates depreciation, using double declining balance method	DDB(1200,100,5,1,5)
EVEN*(number)*	Rounds up to the nearest even integer	EVEN(2.7)
FV*(interest rate, period,payment amount,present value,type)*	Calculates the future value of an investment	FV(1%,15,-100,-800,1)
IF*(condition, value if true, value if false)*	Checks whether a condition is true or false	IF(TRUE,10,20)
INT*(number)*	Rounds a number down	INT(1234.585)
IPMT*(rate,period, periods,present value,future value,type)*	Calculates the interest paid for a payment	IPMT(1,2,3,5000)
ISBLANK*(cell)*	Checks whether a cell is blank	ISBLANK(Z34)
ISERROR*(cell)*	Checks whether a cell has an error	ISERROR(D25)
LN*(number)*	Finds natural logarithm	LN(56)
LOG*(number, base)*	Finds common logarithm to a specified base	LOG(10,2)
LOG10*(number)*	Finds base-10 logarithm	LOG10(100)
MAX*(range)*	Finds largest value in a range	MAX(A1:A12)
MIN*(range)*	Finds smallest value in a range	MIN(B20:D34)

Function	Description	Example
MOD*(dividend, divisor)*	Calculates the remainder after it is divided by divisor	MOD(10,5)
MONTH*(date)*	Finds the month in the date	MONTH("07/07/93")
NOW()	Returns serial number for the current date	NOW()
NPER*(rate, payment present value, future value,type)*	Calculates the number of payments required to pay off a loan	NPER(10%,-200,-2000, -4000,1)
NPV*(rate,range)*	Calculates the present value of a series of cash-flow transactions	NPV(1%,A1:A12)
ODD*(number)*	Rounds up to nearest odd integer	ODD(3.5)
PI()	Returns Pi	PI()
PMT*(rate,periods, present value, future value,type)*	Calculates payment amount required for an investment to be paid off	PMT(10%/12,12,0,2000,1)
PPMT*(rate,period, present value, future value,type)*	Calculates the principal payment being paid during any time period	PPMT(10%/12,10, 0,10000,1)
PRODUCT*(value1, value2,value3,...)*	Calculates the product of values	PRODUCT(12,233,123)
REPT*(text, number)*	Repeats text for a specified number of times	REPT("*",30)

continues

continued

Function	Description	Example
ROUND*(number, num_digits)*	Rounds a value up	ROUND(234.345,2)
SLN*(cost, salvage,life)*	Calculates depreciation, using the straight line method	SLN(1000,500,12)
SUM*(range)*	Calculates the total of a range	SUM(D1:D54
SYD*(cost,salvage,life,period)*	Calculates depreciation, using the sum of years' digits method	SYD(1000,500,10,5)
TIME*(hour, minute,second)*	Calculates serial number of a specified time	TIME(12,0,0)
TIMEVALUE*(text)*	Converts time into a serial number	TIMEVALUE("12:00 PM")
TODAY( )	Returns serial number of the current date	TODAY()
TRUNC*(number, digits)*	Rounds number down to the nearest integer	TRUNC(3.175,1)
WEEKDAY*(date)*	Returns the day of the week	WEEKDAY("01/01/93")
YEAR*(serial number)*	Returns the year within the serial number	YEAR(0.007)

Index

Symbols

- (Subtraction) operator, 94
$ (Dollar sign) absolute reference sign, 97
% (Percent) operator, 94
& (Combine multiple text values) operator, 94
* (Multiplication) operator, 94
+ (Addition) operator, 94
/ (Division) operator, 94
: (Ranges) operator, 94
< (Less than) operator, 77
<= (Less than or equal to) operator, 77
<> (Not equal to) operator, 77
= (Equal to) operator, 77
> (Greater than) operator, 77
>= (Greater than or equal to) operator, 77
^ (Exponent) operator, 94
... (Ellipsis), xviii
3-D charts, formatting viewing angles, 26-27
3-D View command, 26-27

A

absolute references, 97-98
accelerator keys, xvii
active cells, xiv
  displaying, 8-9
active charts, 12-13
active windows, 167
Add Arrow command, 13-14
Add Legend command, 34-35
Add Overlay command, 37-38
Addition (+) operator, 94
addresses, cells, xiv
aligning cell data, 47-49
Alignment command, 47-49
Apply Names command, 144-146
Arrange command, 168
Arrange Icons command, 169
Arrow tool, Chart toolbar, 14
arrows
  adding to charts, 13-14
  after commands, xvii
  deleting from charts, 14-15
Attach Text command, 15-16
attaching
  notes to cells, 9-11
  text to charts, 15-16
automatic page breaks, 132-133
axes
  displaying/hiding labels and markers, 16-17
  scaling, 40-42
Axes command, 17
axis labels, displaying/hiding, 16-17

B

background, sending graphic objects to, 115-116
borders, adding around cells, 1-2
Bottom Border tool, Standard toolbar, 2
Bring to Front command, 111

C

Calculate Now command, 18
Calculation command, 105-108
calculations
  customizing, 105-108
  recalculating worksheet formulas and updating charts, 17-18
Cancel box, xiv
Cell Protection command, 65-66
cells, xiii
  absolute references, 97-98
  active, xiv
    displaying, 8-9
  addresses, xiv
  borders, adding, 1-2
  data
    aligning, 47-49
    applying styles, 66-67
    clearing, 51-53
    copying, 53-56
    cutting and moving, 56-58
    deleting, 51-53
    formatting, 49-51
    protecting, 64-66
  deleting, 3-5
  filling
    down, 149-150
    right, 150-151
    with series, 152-155
  finding, 159-161
  going to, 5-6
  inserting, 6-8
    Clipboard contents between, 61-62
  notes
    attaching, 9-11
    viewing, editing, or deleting, 11-12
  pasting Clipboard contents into, 62-64
  ranges, *see* ranges
  relative references, 99-100
  selecting, 157-158
    multiple, 159
  shading, adding, 1-2

Chart menu commands, *see* commands, Chart menu
Chart toolbar, *see* toolbars, Chart
charting tools, 21-22, 32
charts
  3-D, formatting viewing angles, 26-27
  active, 12-13
  arrows, 13-15
  axes
    displaying/hiding labels and markers, 16-17
    scaling, 40-42
  color palettes, changing, 18-20
  combination, creating, 37-38
  creating, 88-89
    in separate documents, 22-23
  data series, creating/editing, 24-25
  deselecting, 42
  embedded
    creating, 20-22
    moving and sizing, 36
  gridlines, displaying/hiding, 32-33
  legends, 33-36
  main, formatting, 27-30
  objects
    moving, 36-37
    sizing, 43-44
  overlays, 37-39
  protecting documents, 39-40
  selecting entire chart, 42-43
  text, attaching, 15-16
  types, changing, 30-32
  unprotecting, 44-45
  updating after recalculating worksheet formulas, 17-18
ChartWizard, 20-21
ChartWizard tool, Standard toolbar, 21
check boxes, xix
Clear command, 3, 51-53
clearing cell contents, 51-53
clicking, xvi
Clipboard contents
  inserting between cells, 61-62
  pasting into cells, 62-64
Close All command, 86

Close command
  Control menu, 169-170
  File menu, 85-86
closing
  files, 85-86
  windows, 169-170
Color Palette command, 19-20
color palettes for charts,
    changing, 18-20
colors for cell data, changing,
    49-51
Column Width command, 45-47
columns, xiv
  deleting, 3-5
  display options, setting, 82-84
  inserting, 6-8
  selecting multiple, 159
  text, setting as print titles,
    143-144
  widths, changing, 45-47
  see also cells
combination charts, creating,
    37-38
Comma tool, Formatting
    toolbar, 127
command buttons, xix
commands
  Chart menu
    Add Arrow, 13-14
    Add Legend, 34-35
    Add Overlay, 37-38
    Attach Text, 15-16
    Axes, 17
    Calculate Now, 18
    Color Palette, 19-20
    Delete Arrow, 14-15
    Delete Legend, 35-36
    Delete Overlay, 38-39
    Edit Series, 24-25
    Gridlines, 32-33
    Protect Document, 39-40
    Select Chart, 42-43
    Unprotect Document, 44-45
  Data menu
    Delete, 73-74
    Exit Find, 76
    Extract, 75
    Find, 75-76
    Form, 68-69
    Series, 152-155
    Set Criteria, 78-79
    Set Database, 70-71
    Set Extract, 72
    Sort, 80-82
  Edit menu
    Clear, 3, 51-53
    Copy, 54-56
    Cut, 56-58
    Delete, 3-5, 51
    Fill Down, 149-150
    Fill Right, 151
    Insert, 6-8
    Insert Object, 128-129
    Insert Paste, 61-62
    Paste, 63-64
    Paste Link, 117
    Repeat, 155
    Undo, 166-167
  File menu
    Close, 85-86
    Close All, 86
    Delete, 86-88
    Exit, 84-85
    Links, 118-119
    New, 23, 88-89, 183
    Open, 13, 89-90
    Page Setup, 139
    Preview, 141
    Print, 135-137
    Save, 91-92
    Save As, 92-94
    Save Workbook, 185-186
  Format menu
    3-D View, 26-27
    Alignment, 47-49
    Border, 1-2
    Bring to Front, 111
    Cell Protection, 65-66
    Column Width, 45-47
    Font, 49-51
    Group, 114
    Main Chart, 27-30
    Move, 37
    Number, 126-127
    Pattern, 113
    Row Height, 156-157
    Scale, 41-42
    Send to Back, 115-116

Index 197

    Size, 43-44
    Style, 66-67
Formula menu
    Apply Names, 144-146
    Define Name, 146-149
    Find, 58
    Goal Seek, 100-101
    Goto, 5-6
    Note, 10-12
    Outline, 131-132
    Paste Function, 102-103
    Paste Name, 104
    Replace, 59-61
    Select Special, 160-161
    Show Active Cell, 9
    Solver, 109-111
Gallery menu, 31-32
gray, xvii
Macro menu
    Record, 120-122
    Run, 123-124
    Start Recorder, 123
    Stop Recorder, 119-120
Options menu
    Calculation, 105-108
    Display, 83-84, 132-133
    Group Edit, 186-187
    Remove Page Break, 134
    Remove Print Area, 142
    Remove Print Titles, 142-143
    Set Page Break, 133
    Set Print Area, 136, 143
    Set Print Titles, 144
    Spelling, 162-164
    Toolbars, 165
    Workspace, 10, 189
repeating, 155
selecting, xvi-xviii, 124-125
shortcut menu, *see* shortcut menu
undoing, 166-167
Window menu
    Arrange, 168
    Arrange Icons, 169
    document-name, 167
    Freeze Panes, 170-171
    Hide, 171
    New Window, 175
    Remove Split, 178
    Unfreeze Panes, 170-171
    Unhide, 171
    Zoom, 178-179
Control menu box, xv
    closing document windows, 170
    exiting Excel, 85
Control menu commands
    Close, 169-170
    Maximize, 172-173
    Minimize, 173-174
    Move, 174-175
    Next Window, 176
    Size, 176-177
    Split, 177-178
Copy command, 54-56
Copy tool, Standard toolbar, 55
copying
    cell data, 53-56
    graphic objects, 111-112
criteria, setting, 76-79
Currency tool, Formatting toolbar, 127
Custom toolbar, *see* toolbars, Custom
cutting cell data, 56-58

D

data
    aligning, 47-49
    applying styles, 66-67
    clearing, 51-53
    Clipboard contents
        inserting between cells, 61-62
        pasting, 62-64
    copying, 53-56
    cutting and moving, 56-58
    deleting, 51-53
    extracting, 74-75
    finding and replacing, 58-61
    formatting, 49-51
    protecting, 64-66
data forms, 68-69
Data menu commands, *see* commands, Data menu
data series, creating/editing, 24-25
databases
    criteria, setting, 76-79
    data forms, 68-69